THE RAMPARTS OF NATIONS

THE RAMPARTS
OF NATIONS

Institutions and Immigration Policies
in France and the United States

Jeffrey M. Togman

Westport, Connecticut
London

Library of Congress Cataloging-in-Publication Data

Togman, Jeffrey M.
    The ramparts of nations : institutions and immigration policies in France and the United
States / Jeffrey M. Togman.
      p. cm.
    Includes bibliographical references and index.
    ISBN 0–275–97254–2 (alk. paper)
    1. United States—Emigration and immigration—Government policy. 2.
France—Emigration and immigration—Government policy. I. Title.
    JV6483.T64   2002
    325.44—dc21   2001032927

British Library Cataloguing in Publication Data is available.

Library of Congress Catalog Card Number: 2001032927
ISBN: 0–275–97254–2

First published in 2002

Praeger Publishers, 88 Post Road West, Westport, CT 06881
An imprint of Greenwood Publishing Group, Inc.
www.praeger.com

Printed in the United States of America

The paper used in this book complies with the
Permanent Paper Standard issued by the National
Information Standards Organization (Z39.48–1984).

10 9 8 7 6 5 4 3 2 1

For Mary Ellen

Contents

Figures and Tables   ix

Preface   xi

Abbreviations   xiii

I INTRODUCTION   1
1 Explaining Immigration Policies   3

II THE UNITED STATES   25
2 Lazarus Betrayed and Vindicated   27
3 U.S. Immigration Policies in Hard Times   43
4 Cross-Cutting Reforms   61

III FRANCE   77
5 Bienvenue   79
6 French Immigration Policies in Hard Times   97
7 The New Politics of French Immigration   117

IV CONCLUSION   133

8   Immigration Policies in Comparative Perspective   135

Bibliography   145

Index   153

Figures and Tables

FIGURES

1.1   Immigration and Unemployment in France   10

1.2   Immigration and Unemployment in the United States   10

TABLES

3.1   Immigration to the United States, 1970–1979   51

5.1   Immigration to France, 1946–1955   87

5.2   ONI Fulfillment of Employer Requests for Immigrant
Workers, 1947–1948   88

5.3   Immigrants Regularized in France, 1955–1964   92

5.4   Immigration to France, 1955–1964   93

6.1   Unemployment Rate in France, 1970–1979   108

6.2   Immigration to France, 1970–1979   110

7.1   Unemployment Rate in France, 1980–1989   122

7.2   Family Migration to France, 1980–1989   123

Preface

Books targeted predominantly at academic audiences are very peculiar beasts. Many of those who read them have themselves written on the topic in question, or plan to do so in the future. Many readers of such books have seen earlier versions in one capacity or another. In some instances, readers have commented upon preliminary drafts and influenced in ways both small and large the published book. In the end, academic books are very much the product of ongoing dialogues, and the relationship between author and reader is more intimate than it is in most other genres. Those acknowledged in this preface were critical to my writing of *The Ramparts of Nations*, and the gratitude I express here is heartfelt.

For as long as I have been studying immigration, Martin Schain has mentored me in the subject, and his generosity and encouragement have been immeasurable. Youssef Cohen has taught me more than there is space here to recount, and he has never ceased helping me think through issues in this book more rigorously than I would have otherwise. Gary Freeman showed true kindness to a young writer he did not know, reading sections of this book and offering valuable comments. I want to thank several scholars who have graciously read preliminary papers and offered suggestions, including Anthony Messina, Leah Haus, Lonnie Athens, and Ted Perlmutter. When I first started working on questions of immigration as a graduate student, Aristide Zolberg and Herrick Chapman offered suggestions that have influenced this book, and I remain grateful to them. Steven Brams and Jerome Bruner both took the time to teach me how to think critically and how to write about social science, and I greatly appreciate all they have given me. I am very grateful to my colleagues at Seton Hall University, especially Mary Boutilier, Jo Renee Formicola, Abolghassem Sedehi, Joe Marbach, Suzanne Samuels, Sunil Ahuja, and Scott Spitzer, who have supported me in this endeavor. I owe a special debt to my comrades from graduate school and beyond, particularly Melissa Moore, Dermot O'Brien, Skye Gold, Richard Abate, Jillian Schwedler and the late John Vantine. And finally I want to thank my wife Mary Ellen, who inspires me in everything I do, and to whom this book is dedicated.

Abbreviations

ACLU	American Civil Liberties Union
AFL-CIO	American Federation of Labor-Congress of Industrial Organizations
AHEPA	American Hellenic Educational Progressive Association
ANE	Agence Nationale de l'Emploi (National Employment Agency)
CEDETIM	Centre d'Études Anti-Impérialistes (Center for Anti-Imperialist Studies)
CFDT	Confédération Français Démocratique du Travail (French Democratic Labor Confederation)
CFTC	Confédération Français des Travailleurs Chrétiens (French Confederation of Christian Workers)
CGT	Confédération Générale du Travail (General Labor Confederation)
CNPF	Confédération National du Patronat Français (National Confederation of French Employers)
CQ	*Congressional Quarterly*
EEC	European Economic Community
FAIR	Federation for American Immigration Reform
FAS	Fonds d'Action Sociale (Social Action Funds)
FN	Front National (National Front)
FNB	Fédération Nationale du Bâtiment (National Construction Federation)
FNSEA	Fédération Nationale des Syndicats d'Exploitants Agricoles (National Federation of Farmers' Unions)

FO	Force Ouvrière (Workers' Force)
FPB	Fédération Parisian du Bâtiment (Parisian Construction Federation)
HLM	Habitation à Loyer Modéré (Moderate Rent Housing)
IMF	International Monetary Fund
INED	Institut National des Études Démographique (National Institute for Demographic Studies)
INS	Immigration and Naturalization Service
IRCA	Immigration Reform and Control Act
JACL	Japanese American Citizens League
NAACP	National Association for the Advancement of Colored People
NLU	National Labor Union
OECD	Organization for Economic Cooperation and Development
OFPRA	Office Français de Protection de Réfugiés et Apatrides (French Office for the Protection of Refugees and Stateless Persons)
OMI	Office des Migrations Internationales (Office of International Migrations)
ONI	Office National d'Immigration (National Immigration Office)
OSSB	Order of the Star-Spangled Banner
OUA	Order of United Americans
PCF	Parti Communiste Français (French Communist Party)
PS	Parti Socialiste (Socialist Party)
RPR	Rassemblement pour la République (Rally for the Republic)
SGI	Société Générale d'Immigration (General Immigration Society)
UDF	Union pour la Démocratie Française (Union for French Democracy)
UPF	Union pour la France du progrès (Union for Progressive France)

I

INTRODUCTION

Chapter 1

Explaining Immigration Policies

In the second half of the twentieth century transnational transportation and communication technologies improved, and international economic interactions increased, causing global migratory pressures to rise. The advanced industrialized nations of Europe and North America, with their expanding economies and relatively low birth rates, brought in millions upon millions of immigrants. From 1946 to 1998, the United States alone took in over 26 million legal immigrants. Across the Atlantic, France, a country with roughly one-fifth the population of the United States, allowed nearly 5 million immigrants to settle permanently and legally over the same period, basically matching the United States on a per capita basis. Other wealthy nations, such as Canada, Switzerland, West Germany, Great Britain, the Netherlands, and Belgium, together brought in tens of millions of foreigners as well, leading some to refer to the second half of the twentieth century as "The Age of Migration" (Castles and Miller 1993).

The entry policies that governments have put in place to regulate international migration have varied considerably both among nations and over time. At certain historical junctures, some of the world's wealthiest nations virtually begged foreign workers to come. Governments sent representatives to recruit potential migrants in their homelands, offering to pay for immigrants' relocation costs and guaranteeing them jobs upon arrival. At other times, immigrants could not have been less welcome. Numerous states formally banned the influx of immigrant laborers, reinforced and expanded efforts to police points of entry, and conducted mass deportations. In short, advanced industrialized nations share a mixed history of bringing in and keeping out immigrants. These immigration policies are of considerable importance because entry laws have arguably determined the flow of international migrations more than have any other factors (Zolberg 1978).

In this book I explore why nations implement the immigrant entry policies they do, why some governments allow or encourage large-scale immigration while others restrict it, and why some states shift from liberal to restrictive immigration policies and vice versa. My aim is to explain cross-national and longitudinal variation in immigrant entry policies. Thus the primary object of this inquiry concerns those policies that govern the movement of people across international borders. However, policies that govern the incorporation or assimilation of immigrants and their offspring into "host" societies after their arrival are often inextricably linked to entry policies. Thus I intermittently touch on immigrant incorporation policies as well.

My theoretical disposition is to focus on the ways in which political institutions in advanced industrialized nations shape immigration policies. There has been a resurgence of work in political science that focuses on the impact institutions have on political, social, cultural, and economic phenomena (Katznelson 1998; Koelble 1995; Steinmo et al. 1992), and much of this scholarship has centered on public policy outcomes (Dunlavy 1993; Finegold and Skocpol 1995; Hall 1986; Immergut 1992). In this book I explore the possibility of explaining immigration laws by reference to institutional variables. My approach is not mono-causal. Instead, political institutions are conceptualized as an intervening variable, a filter if you will, that helps determine what, if any, influence other factors such as economic conditions and cultural traditions have over a nation's immigration policies. My method is comparative. The case studies in this book suggest that different institutional structures in France and the United States contributed in causally significant ways to the different immigrant entry policies implemented in these two countries.

THE INFLUENCE OF ECONOMIC AND CULTURAL FACTORS

Few contest the notion that economic conditions influence public policies designed to regulate migratory influxes in advanced industrialized nations. That governments have in many instances given weight to economic factors in formulating immigration policies is empirically undeniable. The theoretical controversies that do exist concern exactly how and to what extent economic structures and developments shape immigration policies. Marxian scholars (Castells 1975; Castles and Kosack 1973; Cheng and Bonacich 1984; Petras 1981) have argued that capitalist states have a natural inclination to encourage large-scale immigration because it is a long-term structural necessity of capitalist production and because it confers numerous benefits upon the bourgeoisie. However, in the short term governments may temporarily restrict immigration to prevent crises of capitalism. From a neo-classical perspective, various scholars (Hammar 1985; LeMay 1989; Martin 1980) have held that immigration policies largely reflect normal business cycles, with liberal entry policies implemented during economic booms when demand for labor is high, and restrictive policies put in place during busts when demand for labor is low. Both schools of thought converge on the general proposition that there is a direct positive relationship between economic prosperity and liberal immigration policies. This is one of the most widely held assumptions in the study of immigration, and one of the most compelling. Let us examine it in greater detail.

As a nation's economy expands, it needs more and more workers. Because immigration is an effective mechanism by which modern nations can rapidly increase their labor supply, we would expect them to encourage immigration during periods of economic growth. A failure to import workers during these periods of prosperity can result in labor shortages. A shortage of hands prevents potentially profitable work from being done and slows the national economy. From an economic perspective, liberal immigration policies would seem to be a prudent course of action during prosperous times. Conversely, during recessionary periods we would expect governments to limit immigration. This is because economic downturns decrease the general demand for labor, including the demand for new labor. Moreover, immigration during hard times is believed to confront indigenous workers with mounting competition for a dwindling number of jobs. Some contest this notion of immigrant job competition and argue that most immigrants fill jobs that indigenous workers would refuse to take under any circumstances (Piore 1979). Nevertheless, the perception that immigrants take jobs from indigenous workers puts pressure on state elites to restrict immigration. Immigration is also perceived to swell welfare rolls that are already expanding due to recessionary unemployment, leading taxpayers and welfare recipients alike to complain that foreigners are depleting scarce public services. We could reasonably anticipate that, faced with all these pressures, state elites would implement restrictive immigration policies during hard times.

Much evidence exists to support economic explanations for immigration policies. Several advanced industrialized nations in the postwar era have followed a pattern of adopting liberal immigration policies during prosperous periods and restrictive policies during economically difficult periods. France, West Germany, and Switzerland all recruited large numbers of immigrants during the generally prosperous 1950s and 1960s. Then, in the midst of the economic crisis of the early 1970s, all three of these nations suspended foreign worker entries. As recession persisted and unemployment climbed, France, Germany, and Switzerland maintained their prohibitions on most new immigration. In these cases, it appears that economic conditions were major determinants of immigration policy.

Do these cases attest to a universal pattern of correlation between economic conditions and immigration policies in advanced industrialized nations? Some historical and cross-national comparisons suggest that they do not. In certain instances, nations have restricted immigration in times of prosperity. In 1962, for example, Great Britain passed the Commonwealth Immigrants Act, a measure that greatly restricted the influx of foreign workers at a time of strong economic growth and high labor demand. Even the British Treasury asserted that there was no economic justification for introducing immigration restrictions (Spencer 1997:115). In other instances, governments have pursued policies of large-scale immigration during periods of economic crisis. In the 1970s, the United States allowed legal immigrant entries to increase annually despite the recession, the oil crisis, and rising unemployment. Taken together, these cases testify to two points: Economic difficulties are neither necessary nor sufficient conditions for significant immigration restrictions, and economic prosperity is neither a necessary nor a sufficient condition for permitting large-scale immigration.

Why did economic developments fail to determine immigration policies in the United States and Great Britain? If economic conditions do not drive immigration policies, what does? Can other considerations, either by themselves or in combination with economic variables, account for immigration policy outcomes in advanced industrialized nations?

Numerous scholars (Brubaker 1992; Herbert 1990; Higham 1955; Meissner 1992; Silverman 1992) have argued that the answers to these questions lie in cultural traditions, especially issues of "national identity," that are important determinants of immigration policy. These scholars point out that immigrants are not just factors of production. Rather, immigrants are human beings of various ethnic, racial, and national identities whose arrivals carry significant meanings for receiving countries. National communities are largely defined by whom they include and exclude, and thus they must develop traditions for dealing with foreigners who come to settle on their territories. These traditions for receiving foreigners are conditioned by individual national cultures. Thus cultural traditions, particularly the ways in which nations conceive of themselves, shape immigrant entry policies. In this vein, Doris Meissner differentiates between "settler nations," such as the United States, Canada, and Australia, where membership in the national community is based on civic participation, and "nonimmigrant" nations, particularly European countries, where membership is determined by ethnicity. The former, according to Meissner, are generally inclined to have liberal immigration policies, while the latter tend to implement restrictive policies. Rogers Brubaker follows a similar line of reasoning when he suggests that different traditions of national self-understanding in France and Germany produced radically different laws for attributing citizenship to immigrants in those two countries. In France, according to Brubaker, a state-centered and assimilationist understanding of nationhood is expressed in policies that attribute citizenship to foreigners rather easily. In Germany an ethnocultural and differentialist understanding of nationhood is expressed in policies that make it very difficult for non-Germans to gain citizenship.

Viewed from the perspective of cultural traditions, immigrant entry policies gain a depth and a texture they lack when analyzed only from an economic vantage point. Nonetheless, important questions exist about immigration policy that cultural traditions cannot answer. Why do nations with inclusive traditions enact exclutionary policies and vice versa? For example, it is hard to reconcile the view of the United States as a "settler nation" with the far-reaching exclusionary laws known as the National Origins Quota System that governed U.S. immigration from the 1920s until the 1960s. And in Germany, in spite of the nation's exclusionary traditions of citizenship, the government adopted new laws in 1999 that gave children born in Germany to non-German parents the right to German citizenship, and reduced the period foreigners had to wait to apply for citizenship from 15 to 8 years. Part of the problem here is that most countries have competing traditions, rather than a single, monolithic tradition, concerning national inclusion and exclusion. What we ultimately want to know is why one tradition prevails at any given historical juncture.

Clearly, in spite of their limitations as explanatory variables, both economic and cultural factors influence immigration policies in important ways. My aim in this book is not to discredit these factors as determinants of immigration policies. Rather, I intend to push economic and cultural factors beyond the explanatory limitations delineated here by asking several critical questions. Why do economic conditions seem to determine entry policies in some instances and not in others? Why do inclusive traditions prevail at certain historical junctures, while exclusionary traditions triumph at others? What are the causal mechanisms that translate macro-level factors such as economic and cultural conditions into immigration policy outcomes?

COMPARATIVE RESEARCH QUESTIONS

Taken together, the histories of French and U.S. immigration policies since the end of World War II provide us with a unique opportunity to convert theoretical questions into historically-specific, comparative research questions. Both countries have experienced generally similar economic conditions, particularly from the end of the war until the early 1980s. The two countries have also shared similar, though not identical, cultural traditions for dealing with foreigners who came to settle in their territories. Yet the immigration policies that the United States and France implemented over the second half of the twentieth century diverged dramatically. This book highlights various moments of immigration policy divergence between the two nations, particularly those that occurred under comparable economic and cultural conditions. For illustrative purposes, let us take a preliminary look at one such moment here.

For most of the 1960s, the United States and France enjoyed the fruits of a postwar economic expansion that produced historically high rates of economic growth and low rates of unemployment in much of the industrialized world. France, as part of its recovery program, had been actively recruiting immigrants since the end of the war. These recruitment efforts, along with a series of labor agreements France signed with sending nations, and the state's decision to condone, if not encourage, illegal entries, led to very high levels of immigration. By 1970, over a quarter of a million immigrants were coming annually to settle in France (OMI 1994). This represented a 108 percent increase in entries since 1960, and a 534 percent increase since 1950.

The United States was not as encouraging of immigration during the early 1960s, although piecemeal efforts were made to erode the restrictive National Origins Quota System that governed foreign entries. However, the Immigration Act of 1965 greatly liberalized U.S. immigration laws, and the number of foreigners coming to the country climbed steeply. In 1970, over 370,000 immigrants arrived in the United States to establish permanent residence (INS 1997). This represented a 37 percent increase since 1960, and the largest number of immigrant entries since the National Origins Quota System was put in place in the 1920s. Though the two countries had arrived there by different paths, by 1970 both France and the United States were allowing large-scale immigration.

In the early 1970s, global economic conditions took a turn for the worse. In industrialized nations, the postwar recovery-turned-boom came to an end, as economic growth slowed. Several oil-producing nations of the developing world gained control over petroleum resources within their territories and raised oil prices. The ensuing "oil crisis" rendered energy—the linchpin of modern economies—scarce and expensive. In the United States, real gross domestic product decreased by 0.6 percent in 1974 and by 0.4 percent in 1975, marking the first time since 1946–1947 that GDP had fallen for two consecutive years (U.S. Department of Commerce 1998). In France, economic growth stalled after 1973, and industrial production fell by 8.5 percent between 1974 and 1975 (IMF 1998). Commodity prices became increasingly unstable as well. Inflation in the United States rose from 3.3 percent in 1972 to 11 percent in 1974 (IMF 1998). French inflation more than doubled in two years, rising from 6.1 percent in 1972 to 13.6 percent in 1974 (IMF 1998). A neologism of economic malaise, stagflation, was coined in reference to the combination of stagnant economic growth and high inflation that characterized the period. Concurrently, unemployment in advanced industrialized nations grew. In the United States, the unemployment rate climbed from 3.4 percent in 1969 to 8.3 percent in 1975, while the French unemployment rate rose from 1.9 percent in 1969 to 3.7 percent in 1975 and continued in an upward trajectory to 5.6 percent in 1979 (OECD 1984).

Faced with similar economic difficulties, France and the United States implemented dramatically different immigration policies. As we will see in greater detail in Chapter 2, France reacted to the economic crisis of the 1970s by drastically reducing the number of immigrants it allowed to enter the country. In 1974 the French government announced that it would suspend all further immigration. Citizens from fellow European Economic Community members were exempted from the so-called "immigration ban," and the Constitutional Council limited the government's ability to restrict immigrants who came to reunite with their families. Nonetheless, the immigration ban came close to justifying its unofficial title. Legal entries were cut by over 77 percent, as the number of immigrants admitted by the French state dropped from 255,195 in 1970 to 56,695 in 1979 (OMI 1994). Meanwhile, the United States reacted quite differently to the economic crisis, as Chapter 5 will recount more fully. No one of any influence pushed for restrictions on legal immigration. Instead, the U.S. government allowed legal immigration to increase by over 23 percent, as the immigrant influx rose from 373,326 in 1970 to 460,348 in 1979 (INS 1997). Several important actors did advocate policies that were aimed at reducing immigration by cutting down on the influx of illegal workers, but their efforts failed. No such measures were put in place during the economic crisis of the 1970s.

Statistical analysis confirms what the historical narrative seems to suggest: that the impact of economic conditions on immigration policies was far different in France than it was in the United States. In the French case, a regression analysis (see Figure 1.1) indicates a strong negative relationship between immigration and unemployment between 1962 and 1982. The higher the unemployment rate in France, the lower the number of immigrants the state allowed to enter. As economic explanations would predict, France seems to have followed a pattern of enacting liberal immigration policies during prosperous times and restrictive policies during hard times. In the United States, a far different pattern emerged during the same historical period. A regression analysis (see Figure 1.2) demonstrates a strong positive relationship between immigration and unemployment. Thus, as unemployment rises, so does the number of immigrants admitted by the United States. This is the exact opposite of what economic explanations would predict. The United States has not reduced immigration during hard times.

How can we account for this divergence? Why have economic conditions seemingly shaped immigration policies in France but not in the United

Figure 1.1
Immigration and Unemployment in France

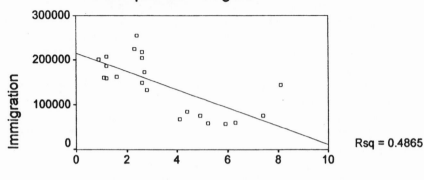

Scatterplot with Regression Line

Rsq = 0.4865

Note: Data from 1962–1982

Source: Adapted from OECD, 1984 and OMI, 1993

Figure 1.2
Immigration and Unemployment in the United States

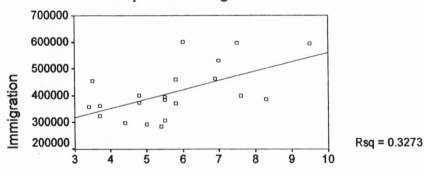

Scatterplot with Regression Line

Rsq = 0.3273

Note: Data from 1962–1982

Source: Adapted from OECD, 1984 and INS 1997

States? Some might contend that different cultural traditions in France and the United States led these countries to enact different immigration policies under similar economic conditions. But this line of reasoning does not hold up well in this instance. France and the United States actually have quite similar traditions for dealing with immigrants. Both nations have brought in massive numbers of immigrants over a very long period of time. While the United States' history of mass immigration is well known, that of France is often overlooked. At various points during the twentieth century, France in fact brought in more immigrants on a per capita basis than did the United States, leading Gérard Noiriel to suggest that immigration carries more economic and social importance in France than it does in the United States (Noiriel 1988:21). Furthermore, both these countries define citizenship expansively and inclusively. Unlike many nations, France and the United States both adhere to the principle of *jus soli* which attributes citizenship to all born within their borders. Both France and the United States have dominant cultural traditions that treat citizenship in terms that are essentially political—one can choose to become French or American— and both reject ethnocultural conceptions of citizenship (Brubaker 1992; Meissner 1992). Of course there are differences in these nations' traditions for dealing with immigrants. Perhaps the most notable is the frequent celebration of immigrant heritage in the United States. But this celebratory tradition failed to prevent the United States from maintaining discriminatory quota restrictions for much of the twentieth century, and the absence of such a tradition hardly inhibited France from becoming a major country of immigration. Overall, we do not find causally significant cultural divergence to which the dramatically different immigration policies enacted by France and the United States might be attributed.

Thus, the question persists: How can we account for this divergence? Taken together, the French and U.S. cases present a puzzle for those interested in understanding why countries implement the immigration policies they do. Why, under quite similar economic conditions, and with quite similar cultural traditions for dealing with foreign migrants, did France and the United States enact radically different immigration policies in the 1970s? In fact, divergence between French and U.S. immigration policies has been the norm since the end of World War II. This book addresses the reasons for this divergence.

THE ROLE OF POLITICAL INSTITUTIONS

I advance the proposition that political institutions play an important role in shaping the immigration policies implemented by advanced industrialized nations, and, in particular, that differences between French and U.S. political institutions go a long way toward explaining the divergence between their immigrant entry policies over the second half of the twentieth century. Political institutions, I suggest, are causal mechanisms that can translate causally-relevant, macro-level forces such as economic conditions and cultural traditions into immigration policy outcomes. Macro-level factors in themselves are only potential influences on immigrant entry policies, and their effects are indirect. Political institutions act as intervening variables that determine which, if any, of these macro-level factors will influence immigration policies, and what that influence will be. Thus, variation in political institutions is critical to explaining variation in immigrant entry policies. Under similar economic or cultural conditions, different institutional arrangements can produce different immigration policies.

Political institutions realize their effects on policy outcomes by shaping interactions among political actors (Hall 1986; Levi 1988; Thelen and Steinmo 1992). Institutions constrain the choices of political actors by making available some courses of action while eliminating other options. Institutions also shape how actors perceive their interests by defining institutional responsibilities and relationships. Finally, institutions affect the power relations among political actors by establishing the degree of influence any one set of actors has over policy outcomes. The way in which political institutions shape power relations is especially critical to the explanation for immigration policies developed in this book. Throughout *The Ramparts of Nations*, I suggest that because institutions affected the power relations among political actors differently in France than in the United States, these two countries followed quite different patterns of immigration policies.

The distinction between actors and institutions can be misleading because certain collective actors—such as political parties, business associations, trade unions, and other important players in immigration policy-making— are institutions in themselves. The term "actors" is used here to denote those entities that engage in goal-oriented behavior. Actors have interests, and they choose courses of action in pursuit of those interests. The term "institutions" refers to those overarching arrangements that influence the choices and interests of political actors, as well as the power relations among them.

Institutional arrangements take both *de jure* and *de facto* forms. They encompass not only codified rules, formal laws, and official governmental structures, but also the informal rules and public codes that structure political interactions. Furthermore, defunct institutions can still influence political interactions. For example, the institution of slavery has shaped political interactions in the United States long after its abolition. Thus, we can say that institutions no longer in place can still have legacies that must be taken into consideration.

The Ramparts of Nations builds upon a growing body of literature in the social sciences that addresses how political institutions influence immigration policy outcomes (Hollifield 1992; Ireland 1994; Freeman 1995;

Money 1999; Tichenor 1994). There is, to be sure, considerable divergence within this genre of scholarship. Gary Freeman, for example, argues that liberal democratic institutions produce expansionist and inclusive immigration policies because these institutional arrangements favor well-organized supporters of immigration, namely employers, over unorganized opponents of immigration, particularly those who compete with immigrants for jobs and government services. Jeannette Money offers a different institutional explanation for immigration policies. She contends that the impact of immigration is mostly local, and that when these specific localities are critical to national elections, immigration issues are tackled. Societal pressures come from regions with large immigrant populations, and these pressures are channeled through political institutions to produce policy outcomes. I address these and other formulations of the institutional hypothesis in the concluding chapter. Here let us note that in spite of differences among authors, throughout this genre scholars claim that political institutions structure power relations among important political actors, and thus help to determine immigration policy outcomes. My analysis of French and U.S. immigration policies proceeds in this vein.

INSTITUTIONS AND IMMIGRATION POLICIES IN FRANCE AND THE UNITED STATES

I have suggested so far that economic and cultural conditions in France and the United States have been quite similar over the last half century, and that the dramatic differences in the immigration policies implemented by these two nations can be attributed in large part to differences in their political institutions and to the ways in which these institutions shape political interactions. This hypothesis needs to be unpacked by addressing several critical questions. What are the differences between these two nations' political institutions? What have been the effects of these institutions on immigration policies? Why have these institutions had the impact they have had on entry policies? I weave my answers to these questions throughout the six historical chapters on French and U.S. international migratory policies. In this introduction I offer a preliminary sketch of my responses to these questions—responses that can only be fully fleshed out through the historical narrative in subsequent chapters.

At the most general level, political institutions in France and the United States are broadly similar. Both countries have maintained liberal democratic systems since the end of World War II, and these institutional arrangements, somewhat ironically, have blunted the influence of the public at large on immigration policies (Gimpel and Edwards 1999; Wihtol de Wenden 1988). This means that public opinion has had little if any sway over entry policies in either country. Instead, political institutions in both France and the United States have allowed only well-organized groups to influence the immigration policy-making process (Freeman 1995). Here, however, most similarities end.

Political institutions in France and the United States have shaped power relations quite differently, and thus the array and composition of organized interests with influence over immigration are not the same in these countries. In the United States, political institutions have produced what is often referred to as a pluralist policy-making process in matters of immigration. A great many interest groups and individuals in the United States compete with one another to determine entry policies through bargaining, negotiation, and compromise (Bentley 1908; Truman 1951). Many see the United States as the pluralist system *par excellence*. One analysis of advanced industrialized countries ranked the United States the most pluralist of all eighteen states in the study (Lijphart and Crepaz 1990).

As subsequent chapters will demonstrate, the United States has allowed a wide array of societal interests—including employers, trade unions, religious organizations, patriotic associations, ethnic-group organizations, and political parties—to participate in the immigration policy-making process. These pluralist dynamics have their roots in overarching U.S. political institutions. The U.S. Constitution has ensured that voluntary associations of all sorts are free to pursue their interests by guaranteeing "the right of people peaceably to assemble, and to petition the Government for a redress of grievances." Moreover, the country's weak party system, separation of powers, and federal structures have, as David Truman (1951) points out, provided multiple points of access through which interest groups can shape public policy.

Political institutions more directly tied to immigration policy have also opened the decision-making process to a plethora of organized interests. Before almost every major decision on U.S. immigration policy in the twentieth century, Congress held extensive formal hearings and allowed a dizzying number of organized interests to participate in the policy-making process. For example, prior to passing the Hart-Celler Act of 1965, Congress heard formal testimony from representatives of the American Legion, the American Coalition of Patriotic Societies, the Daughters of the American Revolution, the Liberty Lobby, the Baltimore Anti-Communist League, the American Veterans Committee, the American Civil Liberties Union, the National Lutheran Council, the Japanese American Citizens League, the National Chinese Welfare Council, the National Council of Agricultural Employers, and the AFL-CIO, among others.

With all this interest group activity in the United States, it is important to note that the state has not been a mere arena in which these organizations compete (Skocpol 1985). Instead, the state has undertaken autonomous action in matters of immigration. More precisely, the state has split into several autonomous actors, each with its own interests, goals, and power basis. The origins of these multitudinous state actors can be traced once again to U.S. political institutions. The U.S. Constitution divided power among the branches of government and established a federal system. As a result, the president has battled Congress over immigration policies, the House of Representatives has fought the Senate, individual states have come into conflict with the federal government, and so forth. As we will see in Chapter 4, when Congress passed the McCarran-Walter Act in 1952 (which basically continued the National Origins Quota System of discriminatory entry policies), President Harry Truman vetoed the legislation, only to have Congress override his veto, and pass the act into law. In the early 1970s, as Chapter 5 will recount in detail, the House of Representatives twice passed bills that would have sanctioned employers who hired illegal immigrants, only to have the bills killed by the Senate. Indeed, the history of almost every major piece of immigration legislation reveals many state actors competing with each other. Overall, we see that a pluralist system created by the country's political institutions has allowed a multitude of both societal and state actors to vie with one another to determine U.S. immigration policies.

French institutional arrangements, on the other hand, are much more difficult to characterize. Many observers have noted that France has a strong statist tradition in which a unitary and autonomous governmental apparatus intervenes in the public sphere without much resistance or competition from voluntary associations in civil society. Over the last half century, French decision-making in the area of immigration policy has indeed shown statist traits, but this fact is not without qualification. Business and labor interests have exerted levels of influence over entry policies that cannot be discounted from either a theoretical or empirical perspective. The interactions among the state, employers, and workers have produced certain corporatist dynamics in the immigration policy-making process. To capture this mix of institutional arrangements and traditions, I refer to the French decision-making process on immigration issues as statist-corporatist. As we will see in Chapter 3, this classification is complicated by the fact that institutional developments since 1981 have chipped away at France's statist-corporatist system of immigration policy-making.

Statism (*étatisme*) has shaped French politics for quite some time. France has a long history of a strong and unitary state apparatus capable of pursuing what elites consider to be the national interest. French political institutions since the *ancien régime* have created a highly centralized governmental system, resisting almost all efforts to separate powers among branches of government or to devolve power to sub-national units. The development and maintenance of a strong state has been abetted by a weak civil society in which there are few voluntary associations that could offset state power. The Le Chapelier Law of 1791 prohibited the establishment of intermediary bodies (*corps intermédiares*), and it remained in force until 1901, greatly damaging all forms of associative life and leaving an institutional legacy that lasts to this day. Short of formal suppression, the ubiquitous French bureaucracy has hindered and preempted autonomous civic coordination and organization, further diminishing the power and proliferation of voluntary associations (Crozier 1964).

Statist institutional arrangements have been particularly pronounced in the area of immigration policy. From the end of World War II until the early 1980s, the French state, or more precisely the executive branch, spoke for the most part with one voice on these issues. There were certainly disagreements among government officials concerning immigrant entry policy, but in the end the state acted quite singularly. The decision-making process for many years was kept out of the potentially divisive parliamentary arena where various interests might express their views on the subject. Instead, the state has implemented its immigration policies via executive decrees and administrative circulars. In fact, between 1945 and 1980, not a single piece of legislation was passed in the National Assembly concerning immigrant entries (Wihtol de Wenden 1988:87).

France's statist institutional tendencies have been tempered by business and labor interests. Over the course of the nineteenth and twentieth centuries, employers and workers were able to establish their own autonomous organizations. In recognition of the importance of these economic interests, government elites have established formal corporatist institutions that have brought the state, business, and labor together to discuss immigration policies. For example, after World War II the French government created the *Office National d'Immigration* (ONI) and granted it an administrative monopoly over immigration. Representatives from the state, business, and organized labor were awarded seats on the twenty-four-member council that ran the agency. Employer and trade union representatives also played important roles on the Economic and Social Council, a body that was charged with, among other things, reexamining French immigration policies in the late 1960s. And in the early 1970s, when French immigration policy fell into crisis, two new corporatist institutions—the National Commission on Foreign Labor and a consultative committee designed to work with the ONI—were created "to involve the social partners [employers and unions] in the elaboration and application of immigration policy" (*Ministère du Travail* 1976). In all these cases, it is important to note not only that business and labor representatives were brought into the policy-making process, but that other organized interests—including religious groups, human rights advocates, and nationalist organizations—were excluded.

The sway of these formal corporatist institutions over French immigration policy should not be overestimated (Wilson 1983). Trade union and employer representation on the ONI was suspended three years after the body was created, and the state was under no legal obligation to follow the recommendations of the Economic and Social Council, the National Commission on Foreign Labor, or the ONI consultative committee established in the early 1970s. But by the same token, we would be ill advised to take an overly formalistic view of France's corporatist dynamics in the area of immigration policy. Informal consultations among government, business, and labor leaders helped to foster what we might call a "spirit of corporatism." Formal corporatist institutions were created partially in recognition of existing, informal corporatist power relations. As we will see in subsequent chapters, the French state's consultation with business and labor leaders has often been ad hoc and reactionary. True to the statist tradition, the French government has frequently formulated immigration policies unilaterally. However, as Peter Hall (1990) has observed for other policy issues, the state has often then unveiled the new policies to affected interests, and, depending on the reaction of the major players, either maintained, modified, or rescinded the policies in question. In the area of immigration policy, the only reactions that the state has heeded, at least from the end of World War II until the early 1980s, have been those of business and labor, adding a corporatist trait to the largely statist decision-making process.

As Chapter 3 will recount, institutional and political developments since the early 1980s have corroded the statist-corporatist nature of immigration policy-making. After taking office in 1981, French President François Mitterrand and his Socialist government enacted new laws that for the first time allowed foreigners to organize politically. Within a couple of years, there were over 4,200 immigrant associations in France (Ireland 1994:63–64). Then, in 1986 Mitterrand and the Socialists converted France's electoral system to one of proportional representation. This allowed the far-right National Front (FN) to win representation—35 seats in all—for the first time in France's National Assembly. The FN had enjoyed some minor successes in regional and European Community elections prior to this point, but it was not until 1986 that the Front truly emerged as a national political force. With the development of immigrant associations and the rise of the National Front, the dynamics of the French immigration policy-making process have been in a state of flux. Statist-corporatist arrangements seem to be giving way to political dynamics that are increasingly pluralist in nature, though it is still too soon to discern whether a full-blown pluralist system is in the making, or to know what the policy ramifications of this shift might be.

To recapitulate the argument to this point, I have suggested that France and the United States, despite similar economic and cultural conditions, have enacted different immigration policies since the end of World War II. On the one hand, France has seemingly enacted immigration policies that correspond to economic developments. France has enacted and maintained liberal immigration policies during prosperous times and restrictive policies during hard times. On the other hand, the United States has implemented policies that seem to be unrelated to economic developments. Indeed, restrictive policies have been maintained during certain periods of economic good fortune, while liberal policies have been kept in place during economic downturns. To account for this divergence, I have put forth the proposition that political institutions are important determinants of immigration policies, and that different institutional arrangements in France and the United States have been at least partially responsible for the differences between these nations' immigrant entry laws. I have offered a preliminary sketch of these countries' institutional dynamics, suggesting that the United States has exhibited a pluralist system while France has had a statist-corporatist system, though one that today seems somewhat eroded.

Moving forward, the crux of the matter is now this: Why have these different institutional arrangements produced such divergent immigration policies? Why have statist-corporatist dynamics in France led to immigration policies that seem to closely mirror economic conditions? Why have pluralist arrangements in the United States brought about immigration policies that have little if any relation to prevailing economic conditions? What are the specific attributes of these two institutional systems that influence entry laws?

The answers to these questions are developed throughout this book. As we will see, the reasons why French immigration policies seem to have fluctuated in accordance with economic developments begin with France's statist tradition. The French government acted relatively autonomously and singularly on issues of immigration. For many years, government officials formulated entry policies in a coherent, technocratic manner, without parliamentary debate or action, and without much concern for public opinion. Largely insulated from public pressures by French institutional structures, public officials viewed international migration, particularly from the mid-1940s until the mid-1980s, as a predominantly economic phenomenon that needed to be managed accordingly. During periods of economic prosperity immigration was to be encouraged, and during hard times it was to be discouraged.

The power of employers and workers made state elites hesitant to implement such policies unilaterally, but the triangular dynamics among these three groups put the government in a strategically advantageous position. Labor unions, generally speaking, favored restrictive policies, while business interests supported a relatively open door. Thus state elites were almost certain to win support from at least one of the social partners regardless of the approach they pursued. As we will see, the state usually refrained from enacting immigration policies that both employers and trade unions opposed. However, government elites did not seek consensus. The support of one of the social partners seemed to suffice. In the end, because the state supported liberal policies during economic booms and restrictions during busts, and because the state could count on support from at least one of its social partners regardless of the policy it pursued, French immigration policies were strongly correlated with prevailing economic conditions over the second half of the twentieth century. Overall, the French state was able to implement immigration policies without many societal constraints, and to the extent that organized groups did enjoy influence, the political dynamics worked in the state's favor.

In stark contrast, U.S. pluralist institutions have negated the impact of economic factors on immigration laws, rendering policy outcomes highly unpredictable. This is in keeping with the notion that in polities with pluralist institutions, "the functioning of the system itself generates unpredictability" (Pizzorno 1981:281). In part, the reasons for this unpredictability can be traced to the sheer number of interests that participate in the U.S. immigration policy-making process. There are so many actors, and so many possible coalitions among these actors, that the interactions among them are intractable. Moreover, these multiple actors have multiple motivations. Many groups that vie for influence over entry policies, such as ethnic organizations and patriotic associations, are moved by noneconomic considerations, further stifling any potential correlations between economics and immigration policies.

Another institutional element that leaves U.S. immigration policies highly unpredictable is the fractured nature of the state. In the United States, government officials do not construct a singular, technocratic approach to the nation's immigration needs. Instead, various state actors have different opinions concerning which direction U.S. immigration policies should take, and they compete over potential policy outcomes. Because such state actors as the presidency, the Senate, and the House of Representatives have their own power bases, each has been able to block policy initiatives. This has produced a level of legislative inertia that has rendered immigration policy less responsive to cultural and economic change than it otherwise might be.

But just because immigration policy-making in the United States is unpredictable, that does not mean it is inexplicable. Political actors in pluralist systems form alliances in an attempt to prevail on questions of immigration. Historically, groups have split into either restrictive or liberal camps, and the policies implemented are directly attributable to the coalitions that support them. Changes in immigration policies are brought about by shifts in the relevant coalitions. The same could be said for the statist-corporatist arrangements in France. However, unlike the French scenario, the pluralist system in the United States is so intractable and inert that it prevents us from knowing under what cultural or economic circumstances either pro-immigration or anti-immigration coalitions will carry the day, or when coalitions will shift.

PLAN OF THE BOOK

This book offers a historical and comparative account of French and U.S. immigration policy-making since 1945. The first three historical chapters follow the U.S. case. Chapter 2 examines U.S. immigration policies, specifically those enacted during the postwar economic expansion. After World War II, restrictive and discriminatory immigrant entry policies, known as the National Origins Quota System, faced two challenges. First, the rise of Nazi Germany and the discovery of the death camps largely discredited the race-based philosophies upon which the National Origins Quota System was based. Second, the United States embarked on a period of unprecedented economic expansion in the postwar era, thus increasing the demand for foreign labor. Yet in spite of these cultural and economic developments, the U.S. pluralist system allowed anti-immigration forces to maintain the National Origins Quota System and reaffirm its standing with the 1952 Immigration Act. It was not until the 1960s that changes in the pro-immigration coalition led to the elimination of these restrictive policies. Two groups that had previously supported the National Origins policies, trade unions and Protestant associations, changed their positions and put their weight behind more liberal entry laws. Moreover, new pro-immigration organizations such as ethnic groups and civil liberties associations entered the scene and pushed to end the National Origins Quota System. Thus, the pro-immigration coalition was larger than ever. In 1965 it successfully worked to pass the Hart-Celler Act, a landmark piece of legislation that offered more liberal and nondiscriminatory immigration laws.

Chapter 3 examines U.S. immigration policies in the 1970s. This decade is particularly interesting for what did not happen. In spite of the recession, rising unemployment, mounting inflation, and the oil crisis, the United States allowed large-scale immigration to continue unabated. In fact, while other advanced industrialized nations such as West Germany, Switzerland, and France were enacting far-ranging restrictions on immigrant entries, the United States allowed immigration to increase over the course of the decade. It is important to note that many in the United States did call for some form of restrictions, particularly sanctions against employers who hired illegal immigrant workers. But pluralist institutions in the United States allowed those forces opposed to restrictions to block such proposals and to maintain the status quo. Even though President Richard Nixon and the House leadership backed employer sanctions, the Senate Subcommittee on Immigration and Naturalization killed the proposal twice without a hearing. A majority of subcommittee members, including Chairman James Eastland, had close ties to agricultural employers who feared such restrictions would inhibit their ability to hire immigrant workers. The fractured nature of the state provided business interests with a stronghold from which it could block immigration policy initiatives. In effect, the U.S. pluralist system, and the interests that operated within that system, negated the potential impact of economic troubles and allowed pro-immigration forces to maintain the status quo.

Chapter 4 surveys developments in U.S. immigration policies during the 1980s and 1990s. The most far-reaching piece of legislation passed during this period was the Immigration Reform and Control Act of 1986. The act was presented as a two-pronged attack on illegal immigration. The first prong consisted of an amnesty that would eliminate many illegal aliens by legalizing them. This turned out to be highly successful as hundreds of thousands of foreigners stepped forward to regularize their status. The second prong was made up of employer sanctions for those who hired undocumented workers. This was intended to discourage illegal immigration by removing the black-market jobs that attracted these workers. However, the sanctions as written into the legislation had no teeth, and thus they did little to reduce the influx of illegal workers. This chapter reveals that U.S. pluralist dynamics required the 1986 act to be acceptable to a great many interests. In the end, even employers supported the new laws.

Chapter 5 examines France's efforts to recruit large numbers of immigrants from the end of World War II until the early 1970s. Immediately following the war, formal tripartite institutions were established, and the state, business, and labor were all in accord that France should bring in massive numbers of immigrants. From a formal perspective, this was the height of France's corporatist dynamic of immigration policy-making. But trade union leaders soon turned to opposition of immigrant recruitment, and the government disbanded formal corporatist institutions. Thereafter, the French government adopted a more statist approach, though employers strongly supported its efforts to bring in foreign workers. Indeed, this chapter will demonstrate how state and business leaders collaborated extensively in the formulation and implementation of France's recruitment program during this generally prosperous period. As part of their recruitment strategy, state and business elites actively encouraged illegal immigration to ensure that France would have the foreign labor they believed it needed. France's recruitment of immigrant workers, both legal and illegal, proved quite successful, and the nation's immigrant population grew precipitously. However, by the late 1960s and early 1970s there were signs that France's tremendous postwar expansion was coming to an end. Furthermore, it became increasingly clear that the large and growing immigrant population was not assimilating easily into French society. In light of these developments, state elites began to question the prudence of large-scale immigration.

Chapter 6 looks at France's dramatic shift from liberal to restrictive immigration policies in the 1970s. The global economic crisis hit France hard. In response, state elites sought to restrict the influx of foreign workers. But the dynamics of France's statist-corporatist system made the transition to restrictive policies a halting one. President Georges Pompidou's government moved to reduce immigration by ending the country's tolerance, indeed encouragement, of illegal entries. Here, however, the limits of statism soon became evident. Both employers and labor leaders opposed the new laws concerning undocumented immigrants, and the state, mindful of the power of its social partners, quickly rescinded the policies. Business opposition to immigration restrictions was predictable, but the trade union stance came as something of a surprise. Labor leaders saw the new laws as harmful to foreign workers who already resided in France—a group the labor movement was actively courting. The absence of formal corporatist bodies was partly to blame for the government's unawareness of labor's stand, and officials took immediate steps to set up new corporatist institutions. As the economic crisis worsened, the French government under President Valéry Giscard d'Estaing quickly reformulated its approach and, after consulting with employers and union leaders, enacted extensive restriction on legal immigration. Though many business leaders opposed such a move, trade unions supported the so-called immigration ban, and the state found itself with sufficient support to maintain the policy. However awkwardly, statist-corporatist arrangements translated economic difficulties into restrictive immigration laws.

Chapter 7 explores how immigration became one of France's most salient political issues in the 1980s and 1990s. From one perspective, this was quite an odd development because little changed in terms of the nation's entry policies. In fact, every successive government over the last quarter century has maintained France's prohibition on most new immigration. Nonetheless, during this period immigration emerged as a privileged object of political manipulation. Politicians, especially those on the far right, have pointed to France's immigrant population as the primary cause of the nation's economic difficulties. Most of the public debate centered on how to treat those immigrants and their children who already resided in France. By the 1990s, first- and second-generation immigrants were growing increasingly frustrated with their lack of economic opportunities. Conflicts between the police and second-generation immigrants exploded into full-scale riots in numerous French cities.

Institutional developments have played an important role in the evolving politics of French immigration over the past twenty years. Chapter 7 demonstrates how institutional changes have eroded the monopoly held by state, business, and labor elites over immigration policy. In 1981, the government of François Mitterrand granted foreigners the right to organize. As a result, immigrant associations multiplied, and the face of immigration politics was transformed. In 1986, Mitterrand altered France's electoral rules to allow for proportional representation. Consequently, the far-right National Front won seats in the National Assembly for the first time and legitimized itself, becoming a national political force to be reckoned with. With its electoral gains and newfound prominence, the National Front structured France's political agenda to a significant extent. The mainstream right and left, which had previously viewed immigration as a more technical issue, now dealt with it as the politically charged issue it had become. How this transformation from a tripolar to a multipolar dynamic affects immigration policies and politics is one of the most pressing issues facing France today.

I suggest to the reader that the remainder of this book may be approached in either of two ways. Certainly, the chapters may be read in numerical order, allowing the reader to follow the historical development of U.S. and French immigration policies one after the other. Alternatively, the reader may choose to pair U.S. and French chapters according to historical periods. For instance, Chapter 2, which covers U.S. immigration policy during the postwar expansion, may be read together with Chapter 5, which deals with French immigration policy during the same period. Similarly, Chapter 3 may be read with Chapter 6, and Chapter 4 may be read with Chapter 7. Each method of approach to *The Ramparts of Nations* has its advantages, and I leave it to the reader to choose.

II

THE UNITED STATES

Chapter 2

Lazarus Betrayed and Vindicated

The United States emerged from World War II an economic and military superpower. The country's rapid economic expansion after the war increased labor demand. U.S. immigration law, meanwhile, still enforced the restrictive and discriminatory National Origins Quota System enacted in the 1920s, prohibiting immigration from many non-European regions. The quota system kept total immigration levels far lower that they would have been otherwise. In light of the Holocaust, and especially after the discovery of Nazi death camps, theories of racial superiority and inferiority upon which the National Origins Quota System was based were widely discredited. After the war, state elites and private interests, motivated by a need for immigrant labor and a rejection of racial and ethnic discrimination, mobilized to repeal the quota system.

The U.S. Congress in the late 1940s undertook a comprehensive review of the nation's immigration laws. But the legislation that was passed in 1952, the McCarran-Walter Act, reaffirmed and perpetuated the National Origins Quota System that had drawn the ire of so many. Opponents of the quota system were able to chip away at the edges of the restrictive and discriminatory immigration policies in the years that followed, but it was not until 1965, with the passage of the Hart-Celler Act, that the National Origins Quota System was finally repealed.

This chapter attempts to explain the vicissitudes of U.S. immigration policies during the postwar period. Why, given the economic and ethical pressure to rescind the National Origins Quota System, did the United States uphold and reaffirm these policies in 1952? Why did the United

States finally repeal the National Origins Quota System in 1965? And to the extent that it helps us explain immigration policy outcomes, we must ask what causally significant factors changed between 1952 and 1965.

I suggest throughout this chapter that U.S. institutional arrangements played a critical role in determining immigration policy outcomes. The fractured nature of the state in the United States prevented any straightforward and unitary action on these issues. In the early 1950s President Harry S. Truman championed the repeal of the U.S. quota system, but he could not persuade Congress to back him. A coalition of Republicans and conservative Democrats in the legislature supported the McCarran-Walter bill, which would perpetuate immigration laws that screened newcomers on the basis of race, ethnicity, and nationality in order to preserve "the bloodstream" of America. Pluralist institutions allowed many organized interests to influence policy outcomes. Numerous so-called patriotic groups lobbied to retain the quota system that would limit immigration from non-European and non-Protestant regions. Several ethnic organizations backed the McCarran-Walter proposal as well, because it would grant token quotas to countries in Asia and other places from which immigration had been banned. The alliance among Republicans, conservative Democrats, patriotic groups, and several ethnic organizations was sufficiently powerful within U.S. pluralist institutional structures to push Congress to retain the National Origins Quota System. The McCarran-Walter Act was passed over President Truman's veto.

By the mid-1960s, two very important developments changed the political landscape of immigration. First, U.S. political institutions still fractured the state apparatus and provided myriad organized interests with access to the policy-making process, but some important groups changed their positions on the issue. Trade unions, most of which supported retaining the quota system in the 1950s, came to oppose the National Origins Quota System in the 1960s, and called for its repeal. Several Protestant associations similarly reversed their positions and opposed discriminatory quotas by the 1960s. Second, new groups entered the fray. Ethnic associations that represented groups discriminated against by the National Origins Quota System lobbied vigorously for its abolition. Thus former supporters and newly active opponents of the quota system joined civil liberties groups and others who had opposed the quota system for quite some time. This expanded coalition of lawmakers and private organized interests was able to push through the Immigration Act of 1965 and eradicate the National Origins Quota System.

IMMIGRATION POLICIES BEFORE 1945

For roughly the first hundred years of its existence, the U.S. government had what amounted to an open door policy. During most of the nineteenth

century, when the government acted on this issue, it was usually to recruit
immigrants who would augment the nation's labor pool and populate its
expanding territory. State officials and employer representatives traversed
Europe in search of potential immigrants (Calavita 1994:56). With the nation's borders open to all willing to come, immigrants flowed consistently
into American territory. From the nation's founding until 1819, an estimated 250,000 foreigners migrated to the United States (Briggs 1984:19).
During the 1820s, the pace quickened somewhat and 143,439 immigrants
came over the course of the decade (INS 1997:25). Then, from 1830 until
1860, the United States received its first wave of modern mass immigration,
as nearly 5 million legal immigrants entered the country. The great majority
of these immigrants were of Irish and German descent (LeMay 1987:21).

The presence of Catholic immigrants from northern and western Europe
in the first half of the nineteenth century provoked a strong nativist reaction
among many Protestant citizens of the urban Northeast, and full-scale riots
broke out in such cities as New York, Boston, and Philadelphia (Briggs
1984:21). This spontaneous anti-immigrant movement became increasingly
organized. In 1845, the Order of United Americans (OUA) was founded.
Its code declared, "Our efforts must be to release our country from the
thralldom of foreign domination" (Bennett 1990:105). After its founding
in New York, this nativist fraternity spread to Pennsylvania, Massachusetts,
New Jersey, Connecticut, and beyond. In 1850 another nativist group
called the Order of the Star Spangled Banner (OSSB) was launched. Many
OUA members joined the OSSB and swelled the latter's membership (Bennett 1990:110). The OSSB were popularly called the "Know-Nothings"
because members were to tell outsiders that they knew nothing about the
secret society. The Know-Nothings formed a political party that did well
in numerous state and local elections, and in 1854 the party elected nine-
teen out of New York's thirty-three congressmen (Bennett 1990:120). The
party's success, however, was short-lived, as the party split on the slavery
issue and the Civil War consumed the nation.

As the war raged on, President Abraham Lincoln proposed a law that
would help bring in more immigrants, and in 1864 Congress enacted the
Act to Encourage Immigration (LeMay 1987:35). The act was the nation's
first comprehensive immigration law at the federal level. It established the
U.S. Immigration Bureau and charged it with promoting immigration. This
legislation was popularly known as the Contract Labor Act because it allowed private employers to recruit foreign workers and sign them to legally
binding contracts. These contracts pledged a worker's wages for up to
twelve months to the employer in exchange for transportation to the United
States and for housing. After the war, organized labor began to lobby
against the Contract Labor Act. The newly formed National Labor Union
(NLU) blamed immigration for the unemployment and depressed wages

that accompanied the recession of 1866–1868 (Briggs 1984:24). The law was repealed in 1868.

Although venomous anti-immigrant sentiment was directed at a variety of ethnic, religious, national, and racial groups, the nation's first restrictive immigration policies were aimed solely at Chinese migrants. Immigrants from China first started to arrive in significant numbers in the 1850s, when tens of thousands came to California, many as aspiring gold miners (Zolberg 1990:316). The California state legislature wasted no time passing anti-Chinese laws, including the 1852 tax on foreign miners and the 1855 head tax on Chinese immigrants. However, the California Supreme Court and the Supreme Court of the United States annulled these taxes. In the 1860s large numbers of Chinese laborers were brought in for railroad construction (Zolberg 1990:317). In 1868, the U.S. and Chinese governments signed the Burlingame Treaty, guaranteeing that Chinese immigrants could enter the United States under the same terms as other foreigners. The treaty met with much hostility in the United States, especially from organized labor. The NLU demanded that the federal government abrogate the treaty and ban Chinese immigration (Briggs 1984:26). In the late 1870s, brutal anti-Chinese riots broke out in California, and the anti-immigrant Sand Lot party elected mayors in both Oakland and San Francisco (Briggs 1984: 26).

In Washington, both the Democratic and Republican parties took up the cause of restricting Chinese immigration. In 1879 Congress passed a bill that would have prohibited immigration from China, but President Rutherford B. Hayes vetoed it, claiming that it violated the Burlingame Treaty. In 1880 China and the United States renegotiated the treaty. Meanwhile, the pressure from organized labor continued to mount. The Knights of Labor rallied their membership against immigration from China and elsewhere, and the Federation of Organized Trades and Labor Unions (a predecessor of the American Federation of Labor, or AFL) passed a resolution against Chinese immigration at its founding convention in 1881. The numerous political parties, labor organizations, and voluntary associations that opposed Chinese immigration finally carried the day in 1882 when the first Chinese Exclusion Act became law. The act was renewed upon its expiration in 1892 and again in 1902, and it was extended indefinitely in 1904.

The ban on Chinese immigration presented Japanese immigrants with work opportunities in the United States. However, restrictionist forces were soon able to close the door to Japanese immigrants. By the turn of the century, newspapers in California were stoking xenophobic fires by warning of a Japanese "invasion," and nativists in the state founded the Asiatic Exclusion League and pressed for a ban on immigration from Japan (Reimers 1992:5). In 1906 the San Francisco School Board decided that Japanese children would have to attend segregated schools (Reimers 1992:5).

The California state legislature joined the fray by adopting a resolution that urged Congress to stop all Japanese immigration to the United States. Tensions between the United States and Japan were already running high due to the dispute over the Hawaiian Islands, and President Theodore Roosevelt recognized that the anti-Japanese actions in California might very well push the two nations to war (Briggs 1984:34). Roosevelt was able to persuade the Japanese government to refuse passports to its nationals (as well as to nationals of Korea, a Japanese colony at the time) who wanted to immigrate to the United States. Roosevelt promised that in return the United States would not formally ban Japanese immigration as it had banned Chinese immigration. Furthermore, Roosevelt was able to convince the San Francisco School Board to refrain from segregating Japanese schoolchildren. This compromise, known as the "Gentlemen's Agreement," was formalized by an exchange of letters in 1908.

In 1917 Congress created the Asiatic Barred Zone, from which foreign labor migration was prohibited. This extended the blanket of exclusion to cover all of India, Afghanistan, and Arabia, as well as parts of East Asia and the Pacific. The act also required all immigrants over the age of sixteen to pass a literacy test in their native language—a measure designed in part to discourage immigration from eastern and southern Europe, where far fewer people were able to read and write than in northern and western Europe. President William Taft in 1912 and President Woodrow Wilson in 1915 had vetoed similar bills, but in 1917 Congress was able to muster the votes necessary to override Wilson's veto and the act became law.

In the 1920s anti-immigration forces enacted a comprehensive and discriminatory system of immigration laws. These laws greatly limited the overall volume of immigration, and assured that those who did come would be predominantly from northern and western Europe. The First Quota Act of 1921 stipulated that the number of visas granted to a given foreign country could not exceed 3 percent of the number of people born in that country who resided in the United States in 1910. So, for example, if there were 100 people who were born in, say, Atlantis living in the United States in 1910, then Atlantis would be granted a quota of three visas each year. Because the great majority of the foreign-born population in the United States came from northern and western Europe, the act guaranteed that most future immigrants would come from the same regions. The 3 percent ceiling capped the total number of visas at 355,000.

For the rest of the decade, restrictionist forces in Congress lowered the total number of immigrants allowed into the United States, and increased the proportion of visas allotted to northern and western Europeans. In 1924 Congress passed the Second Quota Act, which tightened the restrictions to 2 percent of a country's foreign-born population and pushed the benchmark date back to 1890, when northern and western Europeans constituted an even larger proportion of the U.S. immigrant population. The

1924 act also lowered the ceiling for total entries from the Eastern Hemisphere to 165,000. In 1929 Congress passed the National Origins Quota System, which reworked once again the criteria for allocating visas. This new system turned the screw in the same direction. The 1929 laws lowered the overall ceiling to 154,000 visas per year and reserved 83 percent of all visas for northern and western Europeans.

The new laws did not cover immigrants from the Western Hemisphere, and this exemption mitigated the restrictions' impact. An average of approximately 50,000 Mexicans migrated to the United States annually during the 1920s (Calavita 1994:59). Legislators were hesitant to limit intra-hemispheric immigration in deference to a prevalent Pan American ideology concerning such issues (Reimers 1992:7). Moreover, Mexican immigrants could be more easily deported than could their European counterparts, should the need arise (Calavita 1994:59).

Yet in spite of the Western Hemisphere's exemption, the restrictive laws of the 1920s significantly changed U.S. immigration policy. The new laws reduced immigration to the United States, and as a result the rate of immigration during the 1920s was lower than any other decade in a century (Ueda 1994:10). This was quite an accomplishment for restrictionist groups, especially considering the U.S. expansionary economy at the time. Moreover, many restrictionists wanted to alter the national and ethnic composition of immigration. Of particular concern was the increase of eastern and southern European immigrants. Here, too, the restrictionists were highly successful. By shifting the baseline year from 1910 to 1890, the visa quota for Italy declined from 42,000 to 4,000, while Poland's quota went from 31,000 to 6,000 and Greece's dropped from 3,000 to 100 (Briggs 1984:44). Great Britain, meanwhile, was allocated 65,000 visas out of the 154,000 available.

The Great Depression that hit the United States in the 1930s reduced the country's appeal as a destination for immigrants. Poverty and unemployment skyrocketed, and before the construction of New Deal social programs, poor and unemployed persons did not receive much public assistance. Legal immigrants who applied within five years of their arrival for what little assistance was available (usually from state and local agencies) risked deportation as a public charge. Prospects were so poor during the 1930s that more people left the United States than came (Ueda 1994: 32).

U.S. immigration policy remained largely unchanged during this period. In part, this can be attributed to the fact that few people wanted to enter the country. Most quota spots went unused during the 1930s. Also, restrictionist groups had already pushed through most of the reforms they wanted during the prosperous 1920s. The increase in immigration restrictions that one might expect during a depression took place at the margins. Bureaucrats enforced the "likely to become a public charge" restrictions more strictly. Local governmental agencies in cities such as Los Angeles, Chicago, and St. Paul tried to get Mexicans to return to their homeland by offering them such incentives as free transportation.

THE WAR AND ITS AFTERMATH

World War II brought numerous and sometimes contradictory pressures to bear on U.S. immigration policy. There was a strong movement toward more restrictive policies, as government officials placed security issues—both real and imagined—over all other concerns. Some of the wartime immigration restrictions pertained to foreigners who wanted to come to the United States, such as the Smith Act of 1940 that authorized State Department officers abroad to refuse visas to any foreigners they believed might endanger public safety. Most of the new restrictions, however, concerned people who had already immigrated and were residing in the United States. One new law, for example, allowed the government to register and fingerprint all aliens living in the United States. The government also enacted new laws that expanded the classification of who could be deported and that allowed the state to deport aliens to places other than their countries of origin. Perhaps the most infamous wartime restriction on immigrants was the detention of Japanese immigrants and their American-born offspring in concentration camps. By instrument of an executive order, President Roosevelt had 110,000 Japanese Americans evacuated from their homes and imprisoned in West Coast camps. The U.S. judiciary upheld the legality of this policy when it was challenged.

At the same time, the United States encountered economic, ethical, and diplomatic pressures to dismantle the National Origins Quota System and to enact more liberal policies. The war effort consumed much of the nation's labor force and created a shortage of workers in many economic sectors. Employers, especially farmers in the Southwest, lobbied the government to admit temporary foreign workers to fill the void (Reimers 1982: 16). The Roosevelt administration responded by negotiating the *bracero* ("farmhand") agreement with the Mexican government in 1942. The *bracero* program allowed Mexican farmhands to enter the United States on short-term labor contracts. Outside the letter of the law, the Immigration and Naturalization Service pursued administrative strategies that helped assure employers had a sufficient supply of workers. Border patrol agents, for example, often brought undocumented laborers to the Mexican border, had them cross over to the Mexican side, and transported them back as legal temporary workers (Calavita 1994:59–60). The *bracero* program, in both letter and spirit, quickly became a major conduit for Mexican immigration. By 1947, there were roughly 200,000 *braceros* working in the United States. By the time the program was terminated in 1967, a total of

4.7 million Mexicans had crossed the border under the terms of the *bracero* agreement (Ueda 1994:33–34).

The nation's immigration policies presented an ethical dilemma. How could the United States condemn the racist ideology of Nazi Germany while it maintained immigration policies based on racial discrimination? Several domestic groups began to fight against discriminatory immigration restrictions. In 1942 a group of scholars interested in Asia, joined by church leaders and other writers, organized the Citizens Committee to Repeal Chinese Exclusion (Reimers 1982:17). Pearl S. Buck, author of a best-selling novel about China entitled *The Good Earth*, was a founding member of the committee. Congressman Walter Judd, a Republican from Minnesota and an outspoken critic of discrimination, guided the groups' legislative strategy. The goals of anti-discriminatory forces dovetailed with emerging U.S. foreign policy interests. China had become an American ally in 1941, and the United States sought its continued support and that of numerous other states in the Far East and elsewhere whose nationals were also barred from entering the United States. As World War II came to an end and the Cold War began, U.S. elites increasingly saw immigration and naturalization policy as a potential tool for shaping foreign relations and reinforcing alliances (Ueda 1994:42). Those who opposed restrictions for ethical and geo-strategic reasons won a small victory in 1943 when Congress repealed the Chinese Exclusion Act and gave China an annual quota of 105. In 1946 the Asiatic Barred Zone was dismantled and token quotas were given to nations of the region.

With the war won, there was widespread agreement in Congress that the United States needed a comprehensive review of its immigration and naturalization policies. Between 1947 and 1950, the Judiciary Committees of both the House and the Senate conducted an extensive study of the issue. The Senate committee, chaired by Senator Patrick McCarran (D-NV), issued a lengthy report in 1950. McCarran and many of his colleagues in Congress favored the existing quota system, but the legacy of Nazi Germany made it difficult for public figures to use theories of racial superiority to justify discriminatory policies. Instead, those who wanted to maintain the predominantly northern and western European composition of immigration to the United States turned to theories of cultural compatibility. The Senate report claimed that "without giving credence to any theory of Nordic superiority," the National Origins Quota System was still needed to "preserve the sociological and cultural balance in the population of the United States" (Bennett 1966:129).

In 1951 McCarran, along with Representative Francis E. Walter (D-PA), began to advance legislation based on the Senate committee's findings. The McCarran-Walter bill aimed to maintain most of the National Origins Quota System that had governed U.S. immigration since the 1920s. Restrictionists believed that the explicitly racist language of the previous quota system should be eliminated, and that formerly excluded nations should be given token quotas (usually 100 visas). But McCarran and his allies argued that the discriminatory mechanisms that kept the total number of visas low and reserved the great preponderance of available visas for immigrants from northern and western Europe should remain in place. Of the 154,657 visas allocated by the McCarran-Walter bill, 65,351 were to go to Great Britain (including Northern Ireland), while 25,814 were designated for Germany and 17,756 were reserved for immigrants from the Republic of Ireland (CQ Almanac 1952:155).

U.S. institutional arrangements provided both supporters and opponents of the National Origins Quota System with considerable access to the policy-making process. The House and the Senate held a joint hearing on immigration and naturalization issues in the spring of 1951. Several religious and ethnic organizations spoke out against the McCarran-Walter bill. Reverend William J. Gibbons of the National Catholic Rural Life Conference argued in favor of larger quotas for countries in eastern and southern Europe, where many Catholics resided (CQ Almanac 1952:156). Simon H. Rifkind, a former U.S. judge, spoke on behalf of major Jewish groups across the nation and charged that the bills were "restrictive and racially discriminatory" (CQ Almanac 1952:156).

Senators Hubert H. Humphrey (D-MN) and Herbert H. Lehman (D-NY) led an effort to pass a more liberal bill. The Humphrey-Lehman bill would have based the quota system on the 1950 census rather than the 1920 census as the McCarran-Walter bill stipulated, thus giving a somewhat greater number of visas to immigrants from outside northern and western Europe (CQ Almanac 1952:158). The alternative bill would also have made unused visas available to people from other nations and repealed race and sex discriminations (CQ Almanac 1952:158). Altogether, supporters of the Humphrey-Lehman bill estimated that it would allow 50,000 to 70,000 more immigrants to enter the United States annually than would the McCarran-Walter bill (CQ Almanac 1952:158). Various ethnic organizations, including those that represented Greek, Jewish, Lithuanian, Italian, and Polish groups, supported the Humphrey-Lehman bill, as did some small labor associations (CQ Almanac 1952:160).

Nevertheless, there was considerable support for the much more restrictive McCarran-Walter bill. Various patriotic organizations, including the American Legion, Daughters of the American Revolution, and the American Coalition, which brought together ninety-three smaller patriotic groups, were among the most vocal advocates of maintaining most of the National Origins Quota System (CQ Almanac 1952:160). Senator McCarran himself voiced the view of many supporters when he asserted that to eliminate the basic parameters of the National Origins Quota System "would poison the bloodstream of the country" (CQ Almanac 1952:158).

Some who had fought against Asian exclusion supported the McCarran-

Walter bill because it would eliminate explicitly racial criteria for allotting visas, and because it would grant small, token quotas to Asian nations from which immigration had been barred. This is why the McCarran-Walter bill was supported by such groups as the Chinese American Citizens Alliance, the Filipino Federation of America, the Japanese American Citizens League, and the Korean National Association. Representative Walter Judd, a long-time opponent of exclusion, also supported the bill, arguing to his colleagues that to vote for token quotas for these nations was "certainly far better than to vote for total exclusion of them because of their race. Those are your only choices" (CQ Almanac 1952:159).

Although the McCarran-Walter bill had substantial support in both chambers of Congress, the fractured nature of the state gave anti-restrictionists some hope of defeating the measure. In June 1952, Congress passed the bill, but President Harry S. Truman, who had spoken out against discriminatory quotas, vetoed it. Truman denounced the bill in harsh terms, arguing that it would "perpetuate injustices of long standing against many other nations of the world, hamper the efforts we are making to rally the men of East and West alike to the cause of freedom, and intensify the repressive and inhumane aspects of our immigration procedures" (CQ Almanac 1952:159).

But Senator McCarran and Representative Walter had overwhelming support for their bill in Congress, even if some of it was less than enthusiastic. The House overrode Truman's veto on June 26, 1952, by a vote of 278 to 113, and the next day the Senate overrode the veto by a 57–26 vote. Thus the Immigration and Nationality Act of 1952 became law, and the National Origins Quota System, for all intents and purposes, was preserved. The act assembled the nation's disparate immigration laws into a single, uniform code for the first time. The slightly revised method of determining visa quotas was based on the 1920 census and allocated 85 percent of all annual admissions to northern and western European nations (Ueda 1994:43). The McCarran-Walter Act also devised a new preference system that gave first priority to those aliens who had job skills commensurate with the nation's labor needs.

THE HART-CELLER ACT OF 1965

In the 1960s, amidst the nation's reinvigorated civil rights movement, political elites and organized interests led a new drive to eliminate the National Origins Quota System. John F. Kennedy won the 1960 presidential election and immediately became a strong voice in the call for more liberal and egalitarian immigration laws. In the 1950s, he had penned A Nation of Immigrants, a book that celebrated America's "melting pot" history. After he took office, Kennedy asked Abba Schwartz to help him prepare a new admissions formula that would replace the National Origins Quota

System (Reimers 1992:63). In July 1963 Kennedy sent his proposal for immigration reform to Congress. The Kennedy reforms would have granted visas on a first-come, first-served basis and given preferences to those who had special job skills or family relationships to U.S. citizens and residents. But before he could make much progress on this issue, President Kennedy was assassinated in November 1963.

Lyndon B. Johnson, Kennedy's vice president, assumed the presidency. As a senator from Texas, Johnson had supported the National Origins Quota System. In 1952 he had voted in favor of the McCarran-Walter Act, overriding Truman's veto. But once Johnson occupied the oval office he, like Truman and Kennedy before him, pushed to dismantle the National Origins Quota System. In his 1965 State of the Union Address, President Johnson called for an immigration policy based on an individual's job skills rather than racial, ethnic, or national origin.

U.S. political institutions allowed a wide array of societal interests to participate in the debates over immigration policy in the mid-1960s. Ethnic organizations became an increasingly important part of the anti-restrictionist coalition. Several ethnic group organizations had traditionally fought against immigration restrictions, although some had supported the McCarran-Walter Act of 1952 because it removed explicitly racial language and offered token quotas to nations from which immigration had previously been forbidden. But by the mid-1960s, ethnic associations were united behind the call to eliminate restrictive and discriminatory quotas, and they were powerful and effective as never before. Organizations such as the American Committee for Italian American Migration, the National Council of Jewish Women, the American Hellenic Educational Progressive Association (AHEPA, a Greek American association), and the Japanese American Citizens League (JACL) lobbied vigorously in favor of the immigration policy reforms proposed by Kennedy and later by Johnson. The highest political priority for these organizations was to repeal the National Origins Quota System that for most of the twentieth century had discriminated against the ethnic populations they represented. The JACL, which had endorsed the McCarran-Walter Act, now worked to eliminate it. JACL leader Mike M. Masaoka pointed out to members of Congress that under the prevailing admissions system Japan's relatively short waiting list of less than 5,000 migrants would exhaust Japan's visa quotas for the next quarter century (CQ Almanac 1965:476).

Religious groups such as the National Council of Churches of Christ, the National Catholic Welfare Conference, and the Lutheran Immigration Service were also active in pushing for the repeal of the National Origins Quota System. Some of these religious groups were continuing a long history of defending immigrants and refugees. But for others, the fight against the National Origins Quota System represented a complete reversal of position. Protestant groups had long favored restrictions that would preserve the Protestant character of the U.S. population. But by the 1960s, most Protestant organizations opposed discriminatory policies. Donald Anderson of the National Lutheran Council told Congress, "The view of man underlying the national origins quota theory is not too dissimilar from that which ended in tragedy and death for millions in Europe within our lifetime" (CQ Almanac 1965:475)

Perhaps the most significant reversal on the immigration issue could be found among the major trade unions. Trade unions had favored restrictive immigration policies since at least the mid-nineteenth century. But in the 1960s organized labor fought to repeal the discriminatory provisions of U.S. immigration law. James B. Carey of the AFL-CIO gave his "wholehearted support" to the Johnson reforms in his testimony before the Senate, noting that it would "do little or nothing to add to unemployment" (CQ Almanac 1965:475). Trade union support was predicated on the belief that the new laws would not harm American workers, and labor leaders were on the record as stating that the proposed bill would not cause such harm. To assure that the proposed reforms would indeed be innocuous, Carrey and Andrew J. Biemiller, also of the AFL-CIO, asked Congress to add provisions that would assure protection of domestic wages and working conditions. Many of these provisions were included in the bill's final version.

Opposition to the bill came predominantly from groups that wanted to promote an American national identity based on northern and western European origins. Groups such as the American Legion, the American Coalition of Patriotic Societies, and Daughters of the American Revolution were the most active in opposing Johnson's reform proposals. The president of the National Society of Daughters of the American Revolution asked the Senate Judiciary Committee, "Why is it . . . unreasonable to seek to preserve national identity by maintaining the nation's historic population blend?" She further warned that repeal of the National Origins Quota System would lead to "a collapse of moral and spiritual values if nonassimilable aliens of dissimilar ethnic background and culture are permitted gradually to overwhelm our country" (CQ Almanac 1965:477).

Within Congress, Democrats from the South were the main opponents of immigration reform. These so-called Dixiecrats were beholden to constituencies whose forebears came mostly from northern and western Europe and who supported quotas to preserve the existing ethnic and racial proportions of the population (Reimers 1982:37). Representative Maston O'Neal, a Democrat from Georgia, argued that "The supporters of this legislation . . . refuse to accept the fact that human beings differ in their desire to maintain stable governments, their levels of ambition, and their degree of morality" (CQ Almanac 1965:473).

In spite of the efforts of patriotic groups and Southern Democrats, those forces that supported liberal, egalitarian immigration laws had never been stronger, and the National Origins Quota System seemed ripe for repeal. Johnson's Democratic party held roughly two-thirds of the seats in both houses of Congress, and with pivotal Democratic supporters such as trade unions and ethnic associations calling for an end to discriminatory quotas, the majority of Democrats in Congress, save the Southern contingent, stood behind immigration reform. Their control of both the White House and Congress gave pro-reform Democrats a solid grip on the legislative process and the ability to overcome the fractured nature of the U.S. governmental apparatus.

Emanuel Celler, a Democrat from New York and the chairman of the House Judiciary Committee, introduced the Johnson Administration's bill (H.R. 2580) in the lower chamber on January 13, 1965. Two days later Philip Hart, a Democrat from Michigan, introduced the companion bill (S. 500) in the Senate. Both houses held extensive hearings on the immigration reforms, and restrictionists pushed for concessions where they could. In the end, the Hart-Celler Act passed both chambers relatively intact, and President Johnson signed the bill into law on July 4, 1965.

The new reforms represented the most sweeping changes in the history of U.S. immigration policy. Gone was the National Origins Quota System that had assured the great majority of immigration to the United States would come from northern and western Europe. Visas were now granted on the basis of individual qualifications rather than group affiliations, and no country of the Eastern Hemisphere could receive more than 20,000 visas per year. Thus China had the same quota as Great Britain, which had the same quota as every other nation in the Eastern Hemisphere.

While restrictionists lacked the political clout to block the reforms, they were able to extract some modest concessions. For the first time in U.S. history, the 1965 Immigration Act placed a formal limit on Western Hemisphere immigration, set at 150,000 per year. The new immigration system also prioritized family reunion over job skill considerations, reserving 74 percent of all visas for family reunification cases. Because of the combined effects of past migratory patterns and discriminatory admissions policies, potential migrants in Asia and Africa had fewer family members in the United States with whom they could reunite. Restrictionists anticipated that the family reunion preferences they had espoused would lessen immigration from these continents (Reimers 1982:38). In actuality, the 1965 Immigration Act drastically changed the shape of U.S. immigration. With the National Origins Quota System repealed, immigrants came increasingly from Asia, South America, the Caribbean, and other developing regions, and the proportion of migrants coming from Europe dropped significantly. This opening to the developing world helped bring about the largest influx of migrants to the United States since the turn of the century.

CONCLUSION

In the two decades following the war, the United States moved from a discriminatory and restrictive quota system to one that was far more egalitarian and liberal. By 1965 few were willing to stand behind the racially and ethnically biased National Origins Quota System, even if it was now justified in non-racial terms of cultural compatibility. Furthermore, the nation's expansionary economy and low levels of unemployment in the 1960s made the passage of liberal immigration policies more palatable to groups such as trade unions that had previously opposed such measures.

There were no major institutional changes between the 1952 McCarran-Walter Act and the 1965 Hart-Celler Act. Clearly, U.S. institutional arrangements could produce both restrictive and liberal immigration policies. But political institutions played an important role in structuring the interactions that led to the 1952 and 1965 policies. In the early 1950s, the Truman administration wanted to repeal the National Origins Quota System. In the wake of the Nazi regime, there were strong ethical pressures to dismantle the country's discriminatory immigration policies. The postwar economic boom also heightened labor demand. This was partially offset by recourse to Mexican contract labor, but the so-called *braceros* satisfied labor demand predominantly in the Southwest agricultural sector, while other sectors still needed additional workers. Yet in spite of the president's policy goals and ethical and economic pressures, the fractured nature of the state allowed restrictionists in the legislature to defeat Truman's proposals and retain the National Origins Quota System.

In the 1960s the executive branch, first headed by Kennedy and then by Johnson, once again led the charge to dismantle discriminatory and restrictive entry policies. The civil rights movement reinvigorated efforts to repeal laws that discriminated on the basis of race, ethnicity, or nationality. Ethnic organizations that had been divided on the McCarran-Walter Act stood united in their support of what would become known as the Hart-Celler Act. The nation's labor movement also spoke out against the National Origins Quota System, something they had not done earlier. U.S. political institutions allowed myriad societal groups to participate in the policy-making process, and in the 1960s the overwhelming majority of these groups lobbied for more egalitarian and liberal immigration policies. A preponderance of the Congress in both houses also supported such reforms, and thus proponents of more liberal entry policies were able to overcome the fractured nature of the state and pass the Immigration Act of 1965.

While U.S. political institutions proved capable of producing both restrictive and liberal policies, other institutional patterns emerged that seemed relatively consistent regardless of policy outcomes. It was suggested in Chapter 1 that institutions can shape policy preferences, and in the United States there seemed to be an institutional bias by which presidents supported more liberal immigration policies. President Johnson was able to successfully implement Kennedy's initiative to repeal the National Origins Quota System, following in the footsteps of Truman who unsuccessfully fought for similar measures. This pattern can be traced further back. The first attempt by Congress to ban Chinese immigration was vetoed by President Hayes in 1879. Presidents Taft and Wilson vetoed restrictive immigration policies in 1912 and 1915 respectively, only to have Congress override Wilson's veto in 1917 and pass the Asiatic Barred Zone. As a senator from Texas, Lyndon Johnson advocated restrictive policies, and in 1952 he voted to override Truman's veto and perpetuate the National Origins Quota System. But once in the executive branch, Johnson spoke out strongly against discriminatory entry policies and signed the 1965 act into law, reinforcing the notion that there are some institutional rather than merely personal preferences at work here.

Chapter 3

U.S. Immigration Policies in Hard Times

In the early 1970s the extraordinary postwar economic expansion in the United States came to an end. Inflation and unemployment both rose, while economic growth slowed and equities markets fell precipitously. Oil-producing nations successfully pushed petroleum prices to unprecedented highs, and the United States, with its unparalleled reliance on the automobile in particular and on oil in general, was extremely vulnerable to the price increases. By 1974 the United States found itself in a full-blown economic recession.

In response to these disquieting developments, numerous political and societal elites in the United States—including members of Congress, federal officials, trade union leaders, and three successive presidents—called for restrictive immigration policies. More specifically, these elites wanted to see the government act to reduce the number of illegal migrant workers who came to the country each year. The most popular proposals to reduce illegal immigration revolved around placing sanctions on employers who knowingly hired undocumented foreign workers. Such measures, their advocates argued, would protect U.S. workers and legal foreign workers from illegal competition in the labor market. Moreover, supporters of employer sanctions argued that these measures would discourage potential illegal immigrants from coming to the country by eliminating the black-market jobs that attracted them. But in spite of the fact that powerful state and societal interests mobilized in favor of employer sanctions, no such restrictive measures were enacted. In the face of the country's worst economic downturn since the Great Depression, no significant measures to combat illegal entries

were passed, and no measures to reduce legal immigration were even seriously considered. In fact, over the course of the decade, immigration to
the United States, both legal and illegal, increased steadily.

This chapter explores why the United States did not enact restrictive
immigration policies in the 1970s. Certainly, the economic crisis of the
1970s—regardless of whether one conceives of it as a downturn in the
business cycle or as a crisis of capitalism—produced conditions under
which we would expect the United States to restrict immigration. Moreover, there were sociocultural developments that might lead us to predict
restrictive policies as well. After 1965 the ethnic and national composition
of immigrants coming to the United States changed dramatically. By the
1970s, the great majority of migrants were arriving from Asia, Latin America, and the Caribbean. Several analysts cite a lack of cultural compatibility
between immigrants and host societies, and the assimilation problems this
produces, as factors that lead nations to enact restrictive policies. From this
perspective, we might anticipate that the United States, with its European
majority, would limit immigration in the 1970s. These economic and sociocultural reasons to expect the United States to reduce the immigrant
influx in the 1970s are reinforced from a comparative vantage point. Confronted with similar economic problems and with comparable shifts in the
composition of their immigrant influxes, several other advanced industrialized nations—including France, West Germany, and Switzerland—enacted far-reaching immigration restrictions.

Thus the fact that the United States did not enact restrictive immigration
policies in the 1970s, in spite of strong economic, socio-cultural, and comparative reasons to expect it to do so, presents a puzzle of sorts. Indeed,
there were so many reasons to predict that the United States would limit
immigration in the 1970s that, had such policies actually been put in place,
we might be justified in claiming that the outcome was overdetermined.
Rare are the occasions that we ask why certain events did not transpire.
But in this case, where the absence of restrictive policies is so counterintuitive, there are compelling reasons to do so.

This chapter suggests that U.S. political institutions played a critical role
in negating the impact of economic and sociocultural conditions on immigration policy outcomes. Pluralist institutional arrangements allowed a
wide array of societal and governmental interests, many of whom were
motivated by considerations other than the national economic crisis or the
changing ethnic and national composition of immigrants, to participate in
the immigration policy-making process. Moreover, U.S. political institutions created a fractured state apparatus, producing several important state
actors, each with its own interests and power bases. The fractured U.S.
state also provided opponents of immigration restrictions with multiple
points of access through which they could block policy proposals. Thus
U.S. political institutions shaped the interactions among important political

actors in such a way as to allow those who opposed immigration restrictions, particularly employer sanctions, to prevail in the 1970s.

Those who supported immigration restrictions were neither inactive nor few in number. They were just unsuccessful. On the other hand, opponents of immigration restrictions, particularly employer sanctions, were seemingly in the minority. Employers themselves, along with ethnic organizations and civil rights groups that opposed restrictions, faced an uphill battle. But even with every sitting president over the course of the decade, a substantial majority in the House of Representatives, federal agencies such as the Department of Labor and the INS, and the country's largest trade unions all supporting new measures to reduce illegal immigration in the 1970s, the fractured U.S. state provided those who opposed these measures with an alternative stronghold in the Senate from which anti-restrictionists successfully blocked all attempts to curtail the influx of undocumented workers.

THE CHANGING IMMIGRANT INFLUX

From the 1920s until the 1960s, the National Origins Quota System governed immigrant entries to the United States. This discriminatory system reserved the great majority of visas for immigrants from northern and western Europe (see Chapter 2). The Hart-Celler Act of 1965 dismantled the National Origins Quota System and dramatically altered the influx of immigrants to the United States. In the first place, by eliminating discriminatory quotas, the 1965 Immigration Act opened the United States to a far more diverse pool of immigrants. European immigration to the United States had been tapering off despite the National Origins Quota System, but the 1965 act greatly accelerated this process (LeMay 1987:120–125). Europeans constituted roughly 53 percent of all immigrants who came to the United States from 1951 to 1960, 34 percent from 1961 to 1970, and 18 percent from 1971 to 1980 (INS 1999:25–26). In the 1970s the primary sources of U.S. immigration were Asia and Latin America, with a substantial number coming from the Caribbean as well. The act's preference schema also brought more highly skilled and educated workers to the United States than ever before, attracting many of these migrants from India, Korea, the Philippines, and Taiwan (Ueda 1994:62–63). Furthermore, the Hart-Celler Act's emphasis on family migration altered the gender and age balance of the migratory influx, bringing many more women and children to America.

In addition to altering the ethnic and national composition of immigration, the 1965 act significantly increased the overall number of foreigners entering the United States. The National Origins Quota System had reserved most visas for individuals from wealthy northern and western European countries. But the number of people wishing to emigrate from these regions was relatively low. As a result, a great many visas went unclaimed. Between the passage of the McCarran-Walter Act in 1952 and the enactment of the Hart-Celler Act in 1965, almost 40 percent of all available visas went unused (Briggs 1984:62). The 1965 act eliminated this bottleneck and established a "first-come, first-served" system by granting citizens of all nations equal access to visas. The abolition of the National Origins Quota System virtually assured that all of the 170,000 visas allocated to the Eastern Hemisphere and all of the 120,000 visas allocated to the Western Hemiphere would be issued. As a direct consequence of the 1965 immigration act, the annual average influx of legal immigrants jumped from 264,387 between 1951 and 1965 to 424,311 between 1966 and 1980 (INS 1997:25).

In addition to the rise in legal immigration, the flow of undocumented international migrants to the United States also increased significantly after the mid-1960s. The termination of the *bracero* program in 1964 and the enactment of certain provisions in the immigration act of 1965 had the unintended consequence of expanding the illegal influx of foreigners. A great many Mexicans who worked temporarily and legally on American farms under the *bracero* program became illegal aliens when the program was abandoned. The Hart-Celler Act limited Western Hemisphere visas to 120,000 per year and prioritized family migration over labor migration. These two aspects of the 1965 reforms squeezed the number of visas available to immigrant workers from Latin America and elsewhere in the hemisphere. Millions of immigrants ignored these restrictions and entered the country without legal documentation. In the ten years following the 1965 act, the Immigration and Naturalization Service detained and deported roughly half a million illegal aliens annually (Ueda 1994:46). By the early 1970s, most estimates put the number of illegal aliens residing in the United States at somewhere between 1 and 2 million (U.S. Congress 1973:3).

THE PUSH FOR EMPLOYER SANCTIONS

The Hart-Celler Act brought a new wave of immigrants to the United States—a wave that carried more immigrants, both legal and illegal; a wave that was proportionately more female; a wave that had relatively higher levels of education and better work skills; a wave that was more ethnically diverse. At first, the nation's economic prosperity helped ease any opposition there might have been to these new developments. But in the 1970s the United States experienced a severe economic downturn, as what might have been an inevitable downturn in the business cycle was exacerbated by the oil crisis. Inflation rose rapidly, jumping from 3.3 percent in 1971 to 12.3 percent in 1974 (U.S. Department of Labor 2001). Unemployment climbed from 3.4 percent in 1969 to 8.3 percent in 1975 (OECD 1984). Economic growth sputtered as the real gross domestic product decreased by 0.6 percent in 1974 and 0.4 percent in 1975, marking the first time since 1946–1947 that GDP had fallen for two consecutive years (U.S. Department of Commerce 1998). Clearly, a full-blown economic crisis was at hand.

In response to the worsening economic crisis in the United States, influential groups and individuals began to push for restrictions on immigration, especially illegal immigration. Trade unions were the most vocal societal group calling for new restrictions. Union leaders claimed that illegal immigrants took jobs from both Americans and legal immigrants. Howard D. Samuel of the Amalgamated Clothing Workers of America argued that for every undocumented foreign worker in the United States there was "one job opportunity lost to a legal alien or citizen" (*New York Times*, March 3, 1972, p. 58). Labor leaders also charged that undocumented workers were being used by employers as strikebreakers, and that the presence of undocumented workers lowered wages throughout the nation. Testifying before Congress, Sigmund Arywitz of the AFL-CIO stated that an undocumented worker's "real effect . . . is on the lowering of wage standards. He works for less, he is in hiding, he doesn't complain, he doesn't demand what other workers get" (U.S. Congress 1973:12). Of all U.S. workers, African Americans were perhaps the most vulnerable to competition from illegal aliens. The NAACP, citing African Americans' heightened vulnerability to competition from immigrant workers, joined trade unions in pushing for sanctions against businesses that hired undocumented foreign laborers (Gimpel and Edwards 1999:117).

Numerous political elites, especially in the House of Representatives, rallied to the cause of curtailing illegal immigration. Perhaps no public official was more committed to reducing illegal immigration than Representative Peter W. Rodino Jr., a Democrat who chaired the House Subcommittee on Immigration in 1971 and 1972. Rodino, representing a highly industrialized district that included the city of Newark in northern New Jersey, had strong ties to organized labor (Gimpel and Edwards 1999:114). During his tenure as chair, Rodino held extensive hearings on the impact of illegal immigration and on possible ways to combat the influx of undocumented workers. The subcommittee quickly converged on a solution to the problem: sanctions against employers who knowingly hired illegal immigrant workers. The subcommittee asserted, "The incentive for aliens to enter this country illegally in search of employment and for the employer to exploit this source of cheap labor must be eliminated. The imposition of sanctions upon employers is the best method for removing these incentives" (U.S. Congress 1973:22). As the policy-making process moved forward, both the subcommittee and the full membership of the House consistently offered overwhelming support for employer sanctions.

As economic conditions deteriorated, the executive branch added its voice to the call for restrictions on illegal immigration. President Richard Nixon himself spoke out in favor of fines for employers who knowingly hired undocumented workers. Trade unions and labor-friendly members of Congress lobbied the administration vigorously on this issue, and their efforts seemed to bear fruit. During his 1972 reelection campaign, Nixon said illegal immigration "is a problem in which many of our labor organizations are very vitally interested. It does certainly contribute to the unemployment problem" (*New York Times*, June 23, 1972, p. 14). Nixon let it be known that he was prepared to sign an employer sanctions bill into law, and under the direction of his administration, several federal agencies mobilized in support of the bill. Leonard Gilman of the INS told Congress that if sanctions against employers were enacted, "80 percent of our problem would be solved" (U.S. Congress 1973:23). Alva L. Pilliod, also of the INS, warned that without government action, the situation would "get out of control" (U.S. Congress 1973:5). The administration also put forth the claim that illegal aliens were a burden on the nation's welfare system. Joseph Flores of the Department of Labor asserted that undocumented aliens "increase the burden on American taxpayers through added welfare costs—not only by getting on welfare rolls, but also taking jobs which may be filled by persons on welfare" (U.S. Congress 1973:18).

On the other side of this issue, the strongest and most effective societal opposition to employer sanctions came primarily from Hispanic groups and employers themselves, especially those in agriculture. Civil rights groups and disparate religious associations also spoke out against the proposed measures. Hispanic groups feared that the proposed employer sanctions would exacerbate job discrimination. Many believed the proposed bill would push employers to refrain from hiring workers who had Hispanic-sounding names or Spanish accents. In the House of Representatives, Herman Badillo, a Democrat from New York, voiced his objection to employer sanctions and predicted such measures would inevitably "set up a double standard (for employment) with respect to anyone with a foreign accent as the safest way to avoid inquiries by the attorney general" (*CQ* Weekly Report 1972:2403). To avoid the fines, it was feared that businesses would simply stop hiring Hispanic workers, regardless of their residency or citizenship status.

Employers fought quietly but vigorously against the proposed sanctions. Agricultural interests were grappling with the prospect of farm workers' unions and higher production costs, and they turned to illegal aliens in part to keep their costs down (Reimers 1982:47). Employers argued that the measures advocated by Rodino would unjustly put business owners in the role of de facto immigration officers who would have to enforce U.S. immigration laws. Employers also argued that given labor shortages in specific sectors, they needed to rely on illegal workers. In the House of Representatives, members from southwestern states where agricultural employers depended heavily on Mexican migrant workers (legal or illegal) fought to kill employer sanction laws. "We in the Southwest, in Texas, Arizona and

California," Representative Richard White, a Democrat from Texas, told his colleagues, "recognize that at times there is great difficulty in harvesting crops. There is at times a scarcity of labor" (*CQ* Weekly Report 1972: 2403). Together, Hispanic members of the House and members who represented agricultural states were the main opponents of the employer sanctions bill.

In spite of this opposition, there was strong support for employer sanctions, and Peter Rodino was able to pass the bill through the House Subcommittee on Immigration and Naturalization and through the Judiciary Committee. On the floor of the House, support for the bill was overwhelming. A motion to kill the bill by recommitting it to the Judiciary Committee was easily defeated by a vote of 297 to 53. The House of Representatives then passed the bill (H.R. 16188) by a voice vote on September 12, 1972. These, however, were the closing days of the ninety-second Congress, and the Senate did not have sufficient time to consider the bill.

In 1973, with a new Congress in place, Joshua Eilberg, a Democrat from Pennsylvania, became chair of the House Subcommittee on Immigration and Naturalization. He moved quickly to put the Rodino bill (now H.R. 982) back on the agenda for the ninety-third Congress. After holding additional hearings on proposed employer sanctions, the House passed H.R. 982 by a vote of 297 to 63 on May 3, 1973. Thus the bill went to the Senate with overwhelming support from the House of Representatives, with the heads of numerous federal agencies lobbying for its passage, with trade unions and the NAACP speaking out in favor of it, and with the president prepared to sign it into law.

But in the Senate it soon became clear that employer interests had sufficient political strength to kill the bill (Miller 1985:53). This political strength was not widespread, but it was strategically placed within the Senate's institutional structure. Senator James Eastland, a Democrat from Mississippi who chaired the Judiciary Committee and presided over the Subcommittee on Immigration and Naturalization, made sure that the Rodino bill stayed off the Senate's agenda and died a quiet death in committee. Eastland had strong ties to southern agricultural interests, and was himself a cotton planter. The eight-member Subcommittee on Immigration and Naturalization to which the bill was referred had six members from states with strong agricultural sectors: John McClellan from Arkansas, Sam Ervin from North Carolina, Hiram Fong from Hawaii, Strom Thurmond from South Carolina, Marlow Cook from Kentucky, and Eastland himself. Within the matrix of the U.S. legislative process, this eight-person subcommittee had the power to block immigration policy initiatives as it saw fit.

It had never before been illegal under U.S. law for businesses to hire undocumented immigrants. Now, if employers were to be denied access to illegal immigrant labor, agricultural interests wanted to have their access to some form of cheap migrant labor guaranteed. Back in the House, Representative Richard White had proposed an amendment to the Rodino bill that would have allowed employers to hire immigrant workers as temporary contract labor, as had been done under the *bracero* program. But Rodino argued that contract labor would displace Americans, and he had enough support to defeat the motion (*CQ* Weekly Report 1972:2403). Eastland let it be known that before he would allow any employer sanction bill to be reported out of his subcommittee, some form of guestworker program to admit agricultural workers would have to be established (Hohl 1975:61). The vast majority of members in the House of Representatives, as well as trade unions and Hispanic groups, were adamantly opposed to any reinvention of the *bracero* program. Eastland never got his concessions on migrant farm workers, and the employer sanctions bill, twice passed by the House of Representatives by overwhelming margins, never made it to the Senate floor.

In 1975 proponents of employer sanctions tried a new tactic. Rodino attached an amnesty provision to the sanctions bill. The amnesty provision was designed to win over employers and their defenders in Congress who feared that employer sanctions would remove workers from the national labor force without establishing a new guestworker program that trade unions and Hispanic groups adamantly opposed. The amnesty would allow undocumented workers who were already residing in the country to legalize their status. The bill, in essence, would make legal immigrants out of illegal ones, and thus allow them to continue working in the United States. President Gerald Ford supported the bill and stood poised to sign it if the legislation were to come to his desk. Rodino was able to muster enough support to get the bill through the House Judiciary Committee, but the proposal went no further. Having already passed two employer sanctions bills in the previous four years only to have them die in a Senate subcommittee without so much as a hearing, the House leadership never brought the bill to the floor for consideration.

After taking office in 1977, President Jimmy Carter tried to revive the movement to curb illegal immigration. In Carter's first year in the White House, his administration had a bill introduced that combined three initiatives: fines for employers who knowingly hired undocumented immigrants, amnesty for illegal aliens residing in the United States prior to 1970, and increased border enforcement. By trying to give something to everyone, the Carter bill pleased no one and was opposed by both pro-immigrant forces and restrictionists (LeMay 1989:11). Proponents of immigration restrictions were thoroughly frustrated and pushed the issue no further. The decade came to a close without any meaningful restrictions on the number of immigrants coming to the United States during a time of economic crisis.

It would be hard to argue that restrictive immigration policies failed to pass in the 1970s for lack of support. The economic crisis motivated many powerful interests, both public and private, to push for restrictive measures

Table 3.1
Immigration to the United States, 1970–1979

Year	Legal Immigration	% Change Since 1970
1970	373,326	--
1971	370,478	-0.8%
1972	384,685	+3.0%
1973	400,063	+7.2%
1974	394,861	+5.8%
1975	386,194	+3.4%
1976	398,613	+6.8%
1977	464,315	+23.8%
1978	601,442	+61.1%
1979	460,348	+23.3%

Source: INS 1997

designed to curtail illegal entries. Three consecutive presidents, the heads of critical federal agencies such as the INS and the Department of Labor, an overwhelming majority in the House of Representatives, trade unions, and the NAACP all fought in favor of fines for employers who knowingly hired undocumented immigrants. But the fractured nature of the U.S. governmental apparatus provided opponents of restrictions with a critical institutional locus, specifically the Senate Subcommittee on Immigration and Naturalization, from which this minority could effectively veto the proposed immigration restrictions. Economic difficulties drove several organized groups and numerous political elites to support restrictions, but U.S. institutional arrangements allowed opponents to thwart their efforts. Legal immigration to the United States, meanwhile, increased from 373,326 in 1970 to 460,348 in 1979 (see Table 3.1).

TOWARD A UNIVERSAL ENTRY POLICY

The Hart-Celler Act of 1965 was heralded for abolishing the discriminatory entry policies of the National Origins Quota System. Still, all nationals were not handled identically under the new laws. Instead, the 1965 act created two separate entry policies, one for the Eastern Hemisphere and another for the Western Hemisphere. Each hemisphere had its own overall quota, with 170,000 visas allocated to the Eastern Hemisphere and 120,000 to the Western Hemisphere. Each country in the Eastern Hemisphere was limited to 20,000 visas per year, whereas countries in the Western Hemisphere had no per nation limit. In theory, one Western Hemisphere nation could use the entire 120,000-visa allotment.

Perhaps the most important difference between the two policies was the criteria by which immigrants were selected. The Hart-Celler Act devised a preference system for the Eastern Hemisphere that prioritized family migration and skilled labor migration. But the act created no such preference system to regulate the migratory influx from the Western Hemisphere. Instead, visas were distributed on a "first-come, first-served" basis. Thus, would-be immigrants from the Western Hemisphere with relatives residing in the United States or with special work skills had to wait far longer than their Eastern Hemisphere counterparts for visas. By the mid-1970s those who wanted to migrate to the United States from other countries in the Western Hemisphere had to wait approximately two and one-half years for a visa (Hohl 1976:523). The lack of a preference system to facilitate skilled labor migration hurt Canadian citizens the most, since they as a group had higher job-skill levels than their hemisphere's peers. As a result, Canadian immigration to the United States fell from 27,662 in 1968 to 7,308 in 1975 (Hohl 1976:523).

In the 1970s a disparate group of political elites sought to eliminate the discrepancies between the two hemispheres' entry policies. With slight variations, most reformers wanted simply to extend the Eastern Hemisphere system to cover the Western Hemisphere. The primary objectives of their reforms were to facilitate family migration and skilled labor migration from the Western Hemisphere, and to move toward a single, uniform entry policy for all foreign nationals. In 1971 Representative William McCulloch (R-OH) and several of his colleagues introduced a bill (H.R. 2328) on behalf of the Nixon administration that would apply a uniform preference system to both hemispheres, limit nations of both hemispheres to 20,000 visas annually, and grant Canada and Mexico special visa quotas of 35,000 each (Hohl and Wenk 1971:339–341). That same year, Peter Rodino introduced a very similar bill (H.R. 1532) in the House that would also extend the Eastern Hemisphere system to the Western Hemisphere, but his bill granted an even greater exception to Canada and Mexico. The bill placed no numerical limits at all on immigration from these two nations, though they would still be limited by the overall hemisphere quota (Hohl and Wenk 1971:343–348). Edward M. Kennedy introduced yet a third bill (S. 1373), this one in the Senate, to reform immigration policy for the Western Hemisphere by establishing a preference system and a per nation limit of 20,000 visas, again with the exception of Mexico and Canada which would have special quotas of 35,000 each (Hohl and Wenk 1971: 348–356).

The idea of creating a uniform immigration system for both hemispheres faced little opposition. While the McCulloch bill, the Rodino bill, and the

Kennedy bill did not become law in their original form, they demonstrated how widespread the support was for creating a more uniform entry system for both hemispheres. The only significant point of contention was whether Canadan and Mexican nationals should receive special dispensation.

In 1973 the House Subcommittee on Immigration and Nationality, chaired by Joshua Eilberg, held hearings to discuss plans to revise Western Hemisphere entry policies. The Nixon administration actively supported the reforms. Barbara Watson told the committee that the Department of State, on whose behalf she spoke, favored a preference system and per country limits for both hemispheres, as well as special consideration for Mexico and Canada (Hohl and Wenk 1973:327). She further testified that the Canadian government had on numerous occasions expressed to the U.S. Secretary of State its official dismay with the difficulties Canadian citizens had obtaining visas (Hohl and Wenk 1973:326).

The committee eventually combined elements from several proposals into a revised bill that created both a preference system and a 20,000-visa per country limit for the Western Hemisphere, but granted no special status to Canada or Mexico. The lack of any special consideration for America's neighbors to the north and south created some controversy. On the House floor, Rodino sponsored an amendment that would have granted Canada and Mexico special quotas of 35,000 visas each, but it was narrowly defeated by a vote of 203 to 174 (Hohl 1974:69). The bill—without special quotas for Canada and Mexico—went on to garner overwhelming support in the House of Representatives and passed by a vote of 336 to 30 (Hohl 1974:69).

At first, the Senate did not respond to the bill referred to it by the House. One reason for this was that the Senate and its Judiciary Committee were preoccupied with the Watergate hearings. Another reason for the delay was that Senator Kennedy was trying to rally support for his own immigration reform bill (S. 2643), which would have eliminated the separate hemisphere quotas and created a worldwide ceiling of 300,000 (Hohl 1974:70). Meanwhile, Senator Eastland was still holding out for some sort of agricultural guest worker program. Thus the ninety-third Congress adjourned in December 1974 with no action taken by the Senate to reform Western Hemisphere immigration policies.

In spite of the political intrigue, the reforms had widespread support, and it seemed only a matter of time before they were enacted. During the ninety-fourth Congress, the House Subcommittee on Immigration and Nationality once again held hearings on Western Hemisphere immigration policies and wrote a new reform bill (H.R. 14535) that instituted a preference system and a limit of 20,000 visas per country with no exceptions (Hohl 1976:524). The House passed the bill on September 29, 1976, by voice vote. Two days later, the Senate brought the bill directly to the floor by unanimous consent agreement, and the bill was passed by voice vote without debate. On October 20, President Gerald Ford signed the Immigration and Nationality Act Amendments of 1976 into law.

It would be out of line both with the policy-makers' intentions and with the impact of the reforms to interpret the 1976 changes in Western Hemisphere immigration law as restrictive measures. At the time the new laws were passed, Mexico was the only nation receiving more than 20,000 quota visas annually. Thus it was the only nation from which immigration might be reduced by the proposal (Fragomen 1977:95). Even here it should be noted that the visas taken from Mexico would be available to other nations within the hemisphere. Given the tremendous demand for visas and the growing backlog of immigration applications in the Western Hemisphere (297,000 as of January 1, 1973), the visas taken away from Mexico were certain to be claimed by nationals of other countries (Hohl and Wenk 1973: 328). No one believed the 1976 reforms would reduce immigration, and they were right. Instead, it would be most accurate to view the 1976 revisions of Western Hemisphere immigration policies as an attempt to facilitate family reunions and skilled labor migration, and to fulfill the egalitarian aims of the Hart-Celler Act by constructing a global and uniform immigration policy that treated all foreign nationals equally. These efforts were continued, and in some ways completed, in 1978 when Congress passed and President Jimmy Carter signed a bill that created a single system of immigrant entry criteria and combined the two hemispheres' quotas into a single worldwide limit of 290,000.

REFUGEE POLICY

Refugee issues and policies attracted a great deal of public attention in the United States during the second half of the twentieth century. The high visibility of refugee policies has numerous sources. In contemporary times, the mass media—so important in setting the national agenda—has provided extensive coverage of the plight of refugees. Another reason for the high salience of refugee policy is its role in U.S. foreign relations, especially conflictual relations. During the cold war, the United States readily granted refugee status to people leaving communist nations such as the Soviet Union, Cuba, and Eastern Bloc states. By doing so, the United States was symbolically condemning the regimes from which these people fled. Yet another reason why refugee policy is so visible in the United States is that many see the provision of refuge as a hallmark of American political culture. It is part of America's founding myth that the first Europeans to settle in North America were escaping religious persecution, and from this is often derived a national responsibility to provide refuge to others fleeing persecution.

Because refugee issues touch on the nation's founding myth, play a role in the country's conflictual foreign relations, and receive considerable media coverage, the salience of these issues is sometimes disproportionate to their place in the overall context of immigrant entries. Numerically, refugees actually constitute a relatively small part of America's annual immigrant influx. Between 1945 and 1990, of the 18.6 million immigrants who came to the United States legally, only 2.5 million, or roughly 13 percent, were refugees (Ueda 1994:49). To maintain perspective, we should keep in mind that the great bulk of immigration in the second half of the twentieth century consisted of non-refugee entries.

The policies that govern refugee admissions and the granting of asylum represent a unique component of immigrant entry policies—so much so that they may be viewed as a relatively separate policy area. The bulk of non-refugee immigrants to the United States have been admitted either as workers or on the basis of their family relations to U.S. citizens and residents. Refugees, on the other hand, have been admitted because they are fleeing some form of persecution, and there are specific international covenants that deal with the responsibilities of states to provide refuge to those with a well-founded fear of persecution. The distinction between refugees and non-refugee immigrants is not always airtight, nor should it be seen as such. In order to enter a country, an immigrant who wants to work or join family members might apply for asylum to circumnavigate immigration laws. Conversely, a receiving government that wants to limit immigration might deem that a refugee is actually an economic migrant in order to prevent entry. Nonetheless, the distinction is empirically significant. State laws and regulations that deal with immigrants and refugees, as well as the policy processes that lead to these laws, are often quite different.

U.S. political institutions govern refugee policy in a different manner than they do non-refugee immigration policy. Refugee policy has been seen in the United States as part of the nation's foreign policy. Refugee policy has been used to undermine and embarrass regimes hostile to the United States by providing shelter to those who oppose them. U.S. institutions give the presidency a great deal of autonomy in foreign affairs and, by extension, over refugee policy. The executive, through the attorney general's office, can grant refugee status to an unlimited number of immigrants. Thus U.S. refugee policy has largely been an expression of the foreign policy goals of successive administrations.

The most important refugee issues in the 1970s for the United States were engendered by the war in Vietnam. In the spring of 1975 the U.S. military withdrew from Vietnam, dooming the regime it had backed in Saigon to defeat at the hands of the Viet Cong. Hundreds of thousands of Vietnamese who had supported the South Vietnamese regime and fought alongside U.S. troops against the Viet Cong sought to leave the country. As events spun out of control, President Ford used his discretionary power to grant 130,000 Vietnamese the right to enter the United States as refugees

(Gimpel and Edwards 1999:120). The U.S. Congress moved quickly to provide resettlement assistance, job training, and medical care for the refugees.

Some issues often associated with non-refugee immigration arose in the area of refugee policy as well. For example, representatives such as John Conyers (D-MI) and Barbara Jordan (D-TX) feared that Asian refugees would harm the wages and working conditions of African Americans, and opposed proposals to provide public assistance to Vietnamese refugees (Gimpel and Edwards 1999:120). Nonetheless, Congressional deference to the president in this area prevailed, and the support for aiding Vietnamese refugees was overwhelming. In the end, a $405 million assistance package was easily passed in both houses and signed by President Ford. In 1977 a bill to extend public assistance to refugees and to expedite their citizenship applications was passed by Congress without much opposition and signed by President Carter. Overall, the United States welcomed those fleeing Vietnam with open arms; between 1975 and 1979 more than 200,000 Vietnamese refugees were allowed to enter the United States, and they were provided with a considerable amount of government assistance to settle in the country (Reimers 1982:41).

In 1979 President Carter and several congressional leaders spearheaded an effort to reform the country's refugee policy. The influx of Vietnamese refugees, like all previous refugee crises, had been handled in an ad hoc fashion. U.S. immigration law at the time allotted only 17,400 visas annually to refugees. To admit refugees over this numerical limit, the president had to use his discretionary power, which technically resided with the attorney general, to "parole" any additional refugees. Between 1975 and 1979, the attorney general's parole authority was used to admit roughly 250,000 Indochinese refugees (Hucker 1979:1048). The Carter administration sought to develop a refugee policy that could regulate such influxes in a less crisis-driven manner. Introduced in the Senate by Edward Kennedy and in the House by Peter Rodino and by the new chair of the House Subcommittee on Immigration and Naturalization, Elizabeth Holtzman (D-NY), the Carter proposal (S. 643 and H.R. 2816, respectively) would create an annual quota of 50,000 visas for refugees. Refugees from any region of the world, not just communist countries or the Middle East, would be eligible.

Cultural traditions played an important role in the debates over refugee policy. However, as was so often the case, the nation's traditions cut both ways. Proponents and opponents of a more generous refugee policy drew on American cultural traditions in support of their positions. Carter drew on the country's tradition as a haven from oppression. In support of the proposed reform, the president issued a statement that read in part: "Traditionally we have welcomed those who have fled from persecution on account of race, religion or political opinion . . . The United States must continue to honor this tradition as a refuge from persecution" (Hucker

1979:1048). Some opponents of refugee policy reform drew, both implicitly and explicitly, on the nation's tradition of being predominantly an ethnically and racially European country. "Why should we take large numbers of ethnic Chinese when China won't take their own people?" asked Congressman Clarence Long (Felton 1979:1546).

Economic considerations also played a part in the debates. Some feared the economic ramifications of admitting refugees. Virginia Smith (R-NE) held that refugees "go on welfare rolls or they take jobs from our own people" (Felton 1979:1546). But others rejected such arguments. Representative Charles Wilson (D-TX) asserted that refugees "in my district are very hard workers. The people who don't like them don't like to work themselves" (Felton 1979:1546).

Institutional arrangements put the president in the driver's seat on this issue. Even if Congress opposed refugee reform, he could unilaterally admit as many refugees as he wished by instrument of the attorney general's parole authority. Still, Carter preferred to institute a more systematic procedure for refugee admissions. In his State of the Union Address in January 1980, President Carter urged Congress to pass the refugee reform legislation he had initiated, declaring, "I regard its passage as a high priority this year" (Carter 1980:215). Overall, the reforms enjoyed considerable support in Congress. The Senate unanimously approved the bill (S. 643) on September 6, 1979. The House of Representatives passed a similar bill (H.R. 2816) by a vote of 328 to 47 as the first session of the ninety-sixth Congress came to a close in December. After reconciling some small differences between the Senate and House versions of the bill, both houses passed the legislation, and President Carter signed what came to be known as the Refugee Act of 1980 into law.

CONCLUSION

The history of U.S. immigration policy in the 1970s provides a counterintuitive scenario that forces us to question widely-held assumptions and even well-constructed theories about what drives public policy outcomes. The fact that the United States allowed large-scale immigration to continue in the face of an economic crisis of considerable duration illustrates the limits of economic explanations for immigration policy outcomes. Does this mean that economics is not a significant factor in the immigration policy-making process? Clearly not. Economic difficulties in the 1970s, as we have seen, motivated powerful state and societal interests to push for policies that would reduce the influx of undocumented immigrants to the United States. Moreover, the agricultural employers who fought successfully to derail immigration restrictions were also motivated by economic considerations. But what we want to know is why the opponents of employer sanctions were able to defeat this initiative that seemed to have a preponderance of political forces behind it.

Some have suggested that the United States allows large-scale immigration, even when confronted with economic difficulties, because of the nation's cultural traditions. The United States, so the argument goes, is a "settler nation" or a "nation of immigration," one that celebrates its immigrant heritage and welcomes immigrants not merely as supplementary labor, but as new citizens who help populate the nation. Surely there is some truth to this observation. But were these cultural traditions critical to defeating the movement to restrict illegal immigration in the 1970s? The policy-making process delineated in this chapter suggests that they were not. The U.S. tradition of being a nation of immigrants did not prevent three successive presidents, numerous federal agencies, a solid majority in the House of Representatives, and trade unions from supporting measures that they hoped would greatly reduce the number of foreign workers entering the country. Furthermore, the agricultural interests that were able to defeat these measures were not motivated by a desire to protect the country's immigrant heritage, nor did they couch their arguments in such terms. Instead, agricultural interests were motivated in large part by their need for cheap unskilled labor, and their arguments against employer sanctions made this clear.

Others have suggested that the rise of rights-based politics has made it increasingly difficult for liberal democracies to restrict immigration (Hollifield 1992). Some of the evidence examined in this chapter supports this notion. In the 1970s, civil rights were clearly an issue that motivated some opponents of the proposed employer sanctions. Hispanic groups and their advocates argued that if employers faced fines for hiring undocumented workers, they would be more likely to discriminate against U.S. citizens and legal foreign workers who had Hispanic-sounding names or foreign accents, or who somehow looked Hispanic. Civil rights groups like the ACLU argued that employer sanctions would necessitate a national identity card, which they argued was a violation of basic civil liberties. However, although rights-based interest groups opposed employer sanctions, and although employer sanctions were defeated, rights-based interest groups did not ultimately defeat employer sanctions. Instead, as this chapter demonstrates, agricultural interests and their allies in the Senate were the driving forces behind the defeat of employer sanctions.

The key to understanding why the United States did not restrict immigration during the economic crisis of the 1970s is to be found in the nation's political institutions. The most salient institutional characteristic in this instance is the fractured nature of the U.S. state. This fractured state provided opponents of immigration restrictions with multiple points of access through which they could block policy proposals, even with a preponderance of political forces supporting those proposals. In this instance, large farm employers were able to kill the employer sanctions initiative because of the stronghold their advocates had in the Senate Subcommittee on Immigration and Naturalization. In a more unitary state, this could never have happened. Both the executive and an overwhelming majority in the House of Representatives supported restrictions. It is quite possible that a full Senate vote might have passed the proposed bill as well. But in the U.S. institutional system, an eight-man subcommittee was able to prevent a vote by the Senate as a whole, and thus prevent enactment in the 1970s of sanctions against employers who knowingly hired illegal immigrants.

Chapter 4

Cross-Cutting Reforms

For the United States, the 1980s began with an economic downturn marked by high levels of unemployment and negative economic growth. But after the recession of 1981–1982, the U.S. economy rebounded and embarked on an extraordinary period of expansion. Ironically, once the economy started growing at a healthy clip and unemployment was brought under control, the United States enacted sanctions against employers who hired undocumented immigrants as part of the Immigration Reform and Control Act of 1986. The sanctions, which had originally been designed to prevent illegal aliens from competing with U.S. citizens and legal residents for scarce jobs during the 1970s, were repackaged in the mid-1980s as a "law-and-order" issue.

From an economic perspective it seems improbable that such restrictive measures would be defeated during the economic crisis of the 1970s but then be successfully enacted into law during the prosperous mid-1980s. However, U.S. institutional arrangements, and the power relations they shaped, often negated the impact of economic factors on entry policies. As we have seen in the previous two chapters, pluralist institutional arrangements in the United States allowed a great many interests to participate in the policy-making process. Furthermore, the fractured nature of the state provided these interests with numerous points of access from which to influence immigration policy outcomes. Agricultural interests, ethnic organizations, and civil rights groups had successfully defeated any and all employer sanctions proposals during the 1970s. But in the 1980s, supporters of these sanctions were able to pass them by bundling them with other initiatives, particularly a relatively liberal amnesty program for un-documented residents, that won over opponents.

In the mid-1990s, restrictive measures were once again passed during a period of prosperity. In this instance, the impetus for new restrictions came primarily from public officials, especially congressional Republicans. Business interests and other organized groups were able to kill much of what had been an ambitious plan to reduce immigration. Restrictionists settled for legislation that in many respects was symbolic—legislation that seemed to harm and punish immigrants without reducing immigrant entries. Border patrols were increased and reinforced, and many migrants trying to traverse the U.S.–Mexican border were injured and killed due to the increased difficulty of passage (Eschbach et al. 1999). Nonetheless, it remains doubtful that such measures have reduced illegal entries to a significant extent. Furthermore, immigrants' access to public services and their rights to due process in the court system were curtailed. But again, it seems unlikely that these measures have provided real disincentives to would-be immigrants.

THE IMMIGRATION REFORM AND CONTROL ACT

The passage of the Immigration Reform and Control Act of 1986 was the culmination, at least in part, of a long policy-making process that began in the early 1970s. As Chapter 3 recounts, initial efforts to place sanctions on employers who hired illegal aliens failed. When it became clear that Peter Rodino's employer sanctions proposals were going nowhere in the 1970s, President Jimmy Carter tried to make the reforms more palatable by bundling them together with a generous amnesty provision and with increased border control, but his efforts bore no fruit. Unable to pass any significant immigration legislation, Carter and the Congress tabled their reform efforts in 1978 and appointed the U.S. Select Commission on Immigration and Refugee Policy to study the issue.

By the time the Commission issued its recommendations in 1981, Carter had left office and Ronald Reagan was president. The Select Commission's recommendations were quite similar to Carter's bill. They urged policy-makers to "close the back door" to illegal immigrants so that it might "open the front door" slightly to legal immigrants. The Commission reasoned that by fining employers who hired illegal aliens, the government could reduce the underground job opportunities that attracted undocumented foreigners. To deal with illegal immigrants who already resided in the United States, the Commission proposed a general amnesty, on the basis that such a program was preferable to a logistically impossible and politically unacceptable program of mass deportation. Illegal immigration was clearly the leading issue for reformers, and the Hesburgh Commission suggested that only by dealing effectively with the undocumented influx could the country open itself to a widened, yet controlled, legal influx. If illegal immigration were not brought under control, law-abiding immigrants would inevitably suffer.

The 1980s began with an altered political landscape. The Republican party gained control of both the presidency and the Senate. Ronald Reagan and many Republican congressional candidates had run on a platform of fiscal conservatism. The government was the problem, not the solution. In order to spur economic growth, fiscal conservatives called for lower taxes and less government spending. Unencumbered by government interference, market forces would lead the economy to recovery and prosperity. In the meantime, the U.S. economy worsened. In 1982 gross domestic product fell by 2.3 percent compared to the previous year, and the economy fell once again into a recession (U.S. Department of Commerce 1998:151). Unemployment climbed from 7.0 percent in 1980 to 9.5 percent in 1982 and 1983 (OECD 1999:32).

In Congress, Senator Alan Simpson (R-WY) and Representative Romano Mazzoli (D-KY) took the lead on immigration reform in the 1980s, even though neither came from an area with large immigrant populations. These two legislators joined forces beginning in 1981 when they were appointed as chairs of the subcommittees on immigration in their respective chambers. As usual, U.S. political institutions allowed a wide array of interests to participate in the policy-making process. Simpson and Mazzoli held joint hearings of their two subcommittees in September 1981, listening to testimony from numerous political actors, including labor unions, employer representatives, ethnic associations, immigration lawyers, environmental and population organizations, think tanks, religious groups, members of the Select Commission, and many others.

In March 1982, Simpson and Mazzoli introduced an immigration reform bill that reflected many of the recommendations of the Select Commission. Their bill called for employer sanctions and legalization for undocumented workers. Simpson and Mazzoli were cognizant of how agricultural interests had helped kill previous reform efforts, and thus the bill also included major revisions of the H-2 temporary worker program that were intended to placate such opposition by assuring an abundant supply of immigrant labor to agricultural employers (Miller 1985: 60–61). This was precisely the type of measure that agricultural interests and their point man, Senator James Eastland, were demanding in the 1970s, and the refusal of Peter Rodino and labor interests to include such a measure had doomed employer sanctions. By appeasing ethnic groups with the amnesty and agricultural employers with a temporary worker program, Simpson and Mazzoli hoped to succeed where Rodino failed. Furthermore, to ease the opposition of "law-and-order" types to the amnesty, the bill included provisions for stricter border control.

The Senate version of the bill (S. 2222) easily passed in August 1982 by a vote of 80–19. However, a great many opponents of the bill—including

Hispanic groups, trade unions, employers, and civil rights groups—were able to make their voices heard in the House of Representatives. Hispanic organizations and individuals still feared that employer sanctions would lead to discrimination. Representative Tony Coehlo (D-CA) summarized such fears when he told the body, "It is easier to discriminate against someone who has dark hair, dark eyes and dark skin. It is easy to identify those people, and it is easy to assume immediately that those people are illegal and everyone else is legal" (*CQ* Almanac 1982:409). Antonia Hernandez of the Mexican American Legal Defense and Education Fund suggested that the reason the bill had passed easily in the Senate was because, in that chamber, "there is not one single person of color, and it takes a person of color, an Hispanic, a black, to say the things we are saying" (*CQ* Almanac 1982:409).

Business interests also opposed the employer sanctions component of the bill. The Chamber of Commerce argued that such measures would force employers to become immigration officials and to assume the state's responsibility for border control (*CQ* Almanac 1982:409). Civil rights advocates objected to employer sanctions as well, fearing that they might lead to a national identity card (Calavita 1994: 66). Labor organizations opposed the bill on several grounds. First, they did not like the amnesty provisions (Gimpel and Edwards 1999:137). Second, they feared that the temporary worker program would harm workers who were already part of the U.S. labor force (*CQ* Almanac 1982:410).

With all these societal forces lined up against the bill, it stood little chance. The Democratic party controlled the House of Representatives, and many important Democratic backers, such as Hispanics, labor leaders, and civil rights advocates, opposed the Simpson-Mazzoli bill. The Democratic House leadership, especially Thomas O'Neill (D-MA), viewed the bill unfavorably. The leadership allowed the proposal to come to the floor with almost unlimited amendments, a tactic that all but assured the bill's defeat. In a face-saving measure, Mazzoli decided to pull the bill (H.R. 7357) from consideration.

With the start of the ninety-eighth Congress (1983–1984), Simpson and Mazzoli renewed their push for an immigration reform bill that would contain employer sanctions, an amnesty provision, and a temporary worker program. The amnesty provision came under harsh attack. Public opinion had long opposed amnesty for illegal immigrants (Calavita 1994:66). Many conservatives in the House, led by Bill McCollum (R-FL), fought against amnesty, arguing that criminal activities should not be rewarded and that amnesty would generate even more immigration (Gimpel and Edwards 1999:164). Others were worried about the costs associated with an amnesty. As legal residents, those who took advantage of the amnesty would be eligible for governmental services. To ease such objections, provisions were proposed that would delay immigrant eligibility for federal benefits.

Many legislators fought hard to keep some form of amnesty provision in the bill. Although it had been originally proposed to appease opponents of sanctions such as employers and ethnic groups, Simpson and others came to value amnesty as a worthwhile policy in and of itself. They saw illegal aliens as a fearful and exploited subculture that refrained from reporting crimes, seeking medical attention, and protesting mistreatment in the workplace (Gimpel and Edwards 1999:156). Simpson argued that an amnesty would help ameliorate the working and living conditions of these undocumented workers. Representative Larry Smith (D-FL) argued, "We don't want a *sub rosa* economy. It costs a great deal of money to keep that shadow society going" (CQ Almanac 1983:288). Representative Barney Frank said, "I just don't think it is healthy for us to have a large number of people rattling around in illegal status" (CQ Almanac 1983:290).

Hispanic groups continued their fierce opposition to employer sanctions, telling anyone who would listen that that such measures would prod businesses to discriminate against Hispanics and other minorities. Representative Edward R. Roybal (D-CA), chairman of the Hispanic Caucus, prepared hundreds of amendments in an effort to kill the bill. In the summer of 1984, Hispanic delegates and lobbyists mounted a strong campaign against the Simpson-Mazzoli bill at the Democratic National Convention in San Francisco. Presidential candidate Walter Mondale and his running mate, Representative Geraldine Ferraro (D-NY), assured Hispanics that they were opposed to the immigration bill and would do whatever possible to kill it (CQ Almanac 1984:236).

Civil libertarians lobbied against employer sanctions on the grounds that such provisions would require a national identity card, which they abhorred (Miller 1985:67–68). Representative Sala Burton (D-CA) told the House, "The most detestable thing in the world is to have an ID card. The Jews in Europe, in Poland, where I was born, were wearing yellow stars. Is that what we really want?" (CQ Almanac 1984:231).

Since the early 1970s, business interests, especially those in the agricultural sector, had fought against employer sanctions, contending that such measures put employers in the inappropriate role of border patrol. But beginning in 1983, some employers began to change their tactics. Rather than opposing such sanctions outright, employer groups such as the Chamber of Commerce decided to push for a bill that would on balance increase the supply of foreign labor, even if it included sanctions for hiring illegal workers (Calavita 1994:67; CQ Almanac 1983:290).

Agricultural employers, perhaps more than any other group, had been critical to defeating immigration reform in the 1970s. In the 1980s, legislators were making a concerted effort to address their concerns. Agricultural interests wanted secure access to foreign labor, especially seasonal labor. Congresspersons from California such as Pete Wilson (R), Dan Lungren (R), and Leon Panetta (D) worked tirelessly to advance the interests of growers in their state. Panetta proposed a guestworker program that drew harsh criticism from Hispanic groups. Representative Henry Gonzalez (D-TX) called the proposal a "rent-a-slave" program (CQ Almanac 1984: 232). Organized labor strongly opposed the various temporary worker proposals that were floated to satisfy agricultural employers. Legislators tried to work out a compromise that would fulfill agricultural labor demand by expanding the H-2 visa program rather than establishing a new guest-worker policy (LeMay 1989:11–12).

Supporters of the bill in Congress worked hard to push this controversial reform package forward. The measure enjoyed considerable support in the Senate, where the bill was approved in May 1983 by a vote of 76–18. But there was much opposition in the House. Speaker Thomas O'Neill (D-MA) used his control over the House calendar to prevent the bill from coming to the floor in 1983, citing Hispanic opposition as the primary reason for his maneuver (CQ Almanac 1983:287). The bill was reintroduced in the House, and Mazzoli and other supporters of the bill were able to pass it on a 216–211 vote in June 1984. However, the Senate and House versions of the bill were not identical and thus still needed to be reconciled in a conference committee. As election day neared, the Simpson-Mazzoli bill got caught up in presidential politics. The Democratic nominee, Walter Mondale, spoke out against the bill, largely as a bow to Hispanic interests (Gimpel and Edwards 1999:166). In October Congress adjourned, and the 1984 version of the Simpson-Mazzoli bill died in conference committee.

Although the Simpson-Mazzoli bill failed to pass before the ninety-eighth Congress came to an end, it appeared that the immigration reform bill was making progress and gaining momentum by the time the ninety-ninth Congress (1985–1986) opened. Perhaps the most important development was that several members of Congress who protected the interests of the Hispanic population were won over by the bill's supporters. Congressmen such as Bill Richardson (D-TX), Solomon Ortiz (D-TX), and Esteban Torres (D-CA) supported the Simpson-Mazzoli bill during the ninety-ninth Congress. To be sure, they still felt that employer sanctions could lead to discrimination, but these legislators came to believe that the amnesty would be so beneficial to the undocumented Hispanic population in the United States that the trade-off was justified (Gimpel and Edwards 1999:177). To win over Hispanic groups and civil rights associations that feared discrimination against minorities, specific anti-discrimination provisions were proposed, including the establishment of a new office in the Justice Department that would prosecute charges of discrimination that resulted from the sanctions. In the end, five of the eleven members of the Hispanic Caucus supported the 1986 version of Simpson-Mazzoli (LeMay 1989:13–14).

Various provisions in the bill, particularly those that guaranteed farm interests access to foreign labor, won over a significant number of agricultural employers, though not all (LeMay 1989:13–14). The H-2 temporary worker program was to be revised and expanded in order to provide agricultural employers with easier access to foreign labor. Additionally, a program for seasonal workers would give resident status to up to 350,000 immigrants. And the employer sanctions themselves were made more palatable. The sanctions system was constructed in such a way that businesses, by completing some simple paperwork, could easily fulfill their obligations and thereby gain immunity from any possible prosecution (Calavita 1994: 72).

Trade unions had been pushing for employer sanctions for over fifteen years, and they were optimistic that the ninety-ninth Congress might finally enact such a measure. Trade unions also came to support the amnesty, which they now believed would improve working and living conditions not just for illegal workers, but for working Americans in general. The unions strongly opposed some of the concessions made to agricultural employers, but labor leaders saw this as perhaps their best opportunity to get employer sanctions passed. Enacting sanctions was no small accomplishment, for it had never been illegal in the United States for businesses to hire undocumented workers.

The bill (S. 1200) passed the Senate by a 69–30 vote in May 1985. However, it faced a more arduous journey in the House. Labor unions were unhappy with provisions that had been put in place to appease agribusiness. Strong supporters of trade unions such as Peter Rodino (D-NJ) fought against provisions that provided employers with access to large numbers of immigrant agricultural workers. Representatives with close ties to agricultural employers such as Leon Panetta (D-CA) insisted that such measures be included. Unable to resolve these differences, the House had to put off markup until 1986.

In the 1970s, the exclusion of a provision for temporary farm workers led agricultural interests to kill immigration reform in the Senate. In the mid-1980s, it appeared that the inclusion of this type of provision might lead labor interests and their supporters to kill immigration reform in the House of Representatives. However, a small group of legislators, led by Chuck Schumer (D-NY) were able to save the bill by working out a compromise on farm labor that did not include the guestworker program agricultural interests had wanted. With this compromise in place, the Simpson-Mazzoli bill passed through a conference committee, and the joint version of the bill was passed in the Senate by a 63–24 vote and in the House by a 238–173 vote. President Reagan signed the bill, and the Immigration Reform and Control Act of 1986 became law.

The act broke new ground by making it illegal to hire undocumented immigrants and by imposing fines for those who knowingly employed undocumented workers. But in practice the IRCA proved to be one of the more liberal immigration laws in recent history. The employer sanctions provisions turned out to be largely symbolic. By filling out the I-9 form confirming that they had seen documentation of legal status from a worker, employers were deemed as having complied with the law (Calavita 1994: 72). Businesses were not charged with assessing the authenticity of the documents, so compliance was merely *pro forma*. In fact, the I-9 form wound up protecting employers from accusations of illegal hirings. Neither the IRCA nor subsequent legislation ever established a reliable identification system to determine employee eligibility. Perhaps most importantly, there is little evidence that employer sanctions reduced illegal entries. There was in fact an immediate drop in the number of border apprehensions (often seen as an indirect measure of illegal entries), but the reduction appears to have been a consequence of the amnesty, not the sanctions (Calavita 1994: 68–70). This was because many undocumented workers who had been periodically crossing the border, and who were sometimes apprehended, now enjoyed legalized status. When the amnesty program ended, the number of border apprehensions dramatically increased (Calavita 1994:70).

The most significant consequence of the IRCA was the amnesty. Roughly 3 million undocumented immigrants were granted legal status (Tichenor 1994:337). Any illegal alien who had been in the United States since before January 1, 1982, was eligible for legalization. These illegal immigrants had up to a year from May 1987 to apply for legal status. Additionally, certain undocumented immigrant farm workers were also eligible for the amnesty.

THE IMMIGRATION ACT OF 1990

Economic conditions in the United States continued to improve during the second half of the 1980s. Gross domestic product expanded steadily, growing at an average rate of 3.36 percent annually from 1985 to 1989. The unemployment rate fell to 5.2 percent by 1989 (U.S. Department of Commerce 1998; OECD 1999). With the IRCA, which dealt primarily with illegal immigration, finally in place, several Congressional leaders turned their attention to issues of legal immigration. These legislators were spurred on by employers and by European ethnic associations.

Business associations decried the dearth of visas for skilled workers who wanted to migrate for economic motives. The Hart-Celler Act of 1965, which was still in effect, devoted only 5 percent of all visas to individuals with needed labor skills. Virgina Thomas, a lobbyist for the U.S. Chamber of Commerce, argued that the system was "very inflexible and archaic," and failed to "respond to business needs" (*CQ* Almanac 1989:267). Business leaders urged politicians to offer a substantial number of visas to so-called independent immigrants, who would be allowed to enter on the basis of their work skills rather than their family relationships to U.S. citizens or permanent residents.

European ethnic organizations contended that the 1965 act had inadvertently excluded most European migrants. The Irish Immigration Reform

Movement was especially vocal on this front, complaining that the Hart-Celler Act had adversely affected the ability of their compatriots to come to the United States legally (Reimers 1992:253). The Irish economy had suffered considerably during the 1980s, leading many Irish nationals to migrate to the United States, legally or otherwise. By the late 1980s it was estimated that as many as 100,000 Irish citizens were living illegally in the United States (Reimers 1992:253). Edward Kennedy (D-MA), with a large Irish American constituency, was particularly supportive of the effort to increase the number of visas for "underrepresented" European nationals (Gimpel and Edwards 1999:186). On the other side, Hispanic and Asian American groups feared that any changes might limit their ability to bring relatives to the United States. Representatives from these ethnic-based organizations spoke out against proposals to reduce the number of visas allocated to siblings of U.S. citizens and permanent residents. Melinda Yee, executive director of the Organization of Chinese Americans, told Congress, "We consider the nuclear family as also including brothers and sisters" (CQ Almanac 1989:267). Representatives of the Mexican American Legal Defense and Educational Fund, as well as the National Council of La Raza, expressed similar views.

In 1988 Kennedy and Simpson joined forces to advance legislation that would increase the number of skilled immigrants allowed to enter the United States. The Kennedy-Simpson bill set aside 55,000 visas for economic migrants. The visas were to be allocated in accordance with a system that awarded "points" based on education, work skills, age, work experience, and English language proficiency (Reimers 1992:255–256). By design, all these stipulations would favor European immigrants. The bill passed easily in the Senate by a vote of 88 to 4 on March 15. However, Asian and Hispanic groups opposed the bill because it eliminated the fifth preference, which was used by many Asian Americans and Hispanics to bring their siblings into the country. In light of this opposition, the House took no action on the proposal as the 100th Congress came to a close.

In the 101st Congress, Simpson and Kennedy accommodated opponents by restoring the fifth preference to their bill and by making other modifications. Thus a slightly altered version of their bill passed the Senate by an 88 to 9 vote and the House by a 264 to 118 vote. President George Bush signed the bill into law on November 29, 1990.

The Immigration Act of 1990 was a liberal policy that would allow legal immigration to climb from roughly 500,000 to 700,000 individuals per year—a number that was to decrease to 675,000 after three years. The preference system was reduced to three general categories: one for family-based migration (approximately 74 percent of all visas), one for employment-related migration (20 percent), and one for migration from "underrepresented" countries. The category of visas for economic purposes received the largest increase, jumping from 54,000 to 140,000. The legislation left in place the unlimited visa provision for immediate relatives of U.S. citizens. Economic visas were to be allocated on a point system, but the English language proficiency points were eliminated from the final bill. In part, the English proficiency provision was deleted in deference to Asian, Hispanic, and other ethnic groups. The country's historical legacy also played a role in many legislators' opposition to policies that would turn away non-English speakers. Senator Paul Simon (D-IL) said, "Let's not change the American tradition" (CQ Almanac 1989:268). The 1990 act reserved 40,000 places (increased to 55,000 after three years) for countries that were "underrepresented" in U.S. immigration as a result of the 1965 act. An amnesty was included for undocumented family members of immigrants who had been legalized under the IRCA provisions. The act also lifted the immigration ban on homosexuals and individuals who had at one time been members of a communist group.

Overall, the 1990 act had strong support from many powerful organized interests, and this helped account for its passage. Asian American, Hispanic, and Irish American organizations supported the new policy, as did religious, labor, and business groups (CQ Almanac 1990:474). Of course, some did oppose the new measures. Representative John Bryant (D-TX) fought vigorously against the act, arguing, "We have a shortage of jobs and training, not a shortage of people" (CQ Almanac 1990:479). Several Republican legislators signed a dissenting document, citing polls that demonstrated a majority of Americans opposed increased immigration. But as has often been the case, liberal democratic institutions negated the impact of the public at large on immigration policies. In the end, a coalition of well-organized interests and public officials, empowered by the nation's political institutions, successfully pushed for a significant liberalization of U.S. entry policies.

THE ILLEGAL IMMIGRATION REFORM AND INDIVIDUAL RESPONSIBILITY ACT

The Immigration Act of 1990 established the U.S. Commission on Immigration Reform. This commission was modeled after a similar one that had been established in 1978 and headed by Theodore Hesburgh. President Bill Clinton appointed Barbara Jordan, a former congresswoman from Texas, chair of the new commission in 1993. Her reputation as a skilled and fair lawmaker made her appointment widely acceptable. Because Jordan was a Democrat, any charges that the commission was overly beholden to the Republican-dominated Congress were preempted. Because Jordan was African American, any accusations that the commission or its recommendations were racist were also nipped in the bud. There were an estimated 4 million undocumented immigrants residing in the United States, with 300,000 more arriving each year (CQ Almanac 1996:5–4). In this context, the commission was originally designed to study illegal immigration. However, at the insistence of Alan Simpson and others, its competence was later widened to consider legal entries as well.

The Jordan Commission's findings helped set the agenda for immigration reform in the 1990s. The commission issued two reports, the first in 1994 and the second in 1995. The commission contended that the only way to reduce illegal immigration was to prevent employers from hiring undocumented workers. In order to tackle the problem of illegal workers, the commission recommended several measures, including the controversial establishment of a computerized registry of all Social Security numbers that would allow employers to verify worker eligibility. The commission also recommended reforming the selection criteria once again. Members were particularly concerned by the backlogs of would-be immigrants who were immediate relatives of legal residents. The commission urged that preference categories for non nuclear family members be eliminated, and that these visas be transferred to the nuclear family member quotas.

In the 1994 elections, the Republican Party wrested control from the Democrats of both the House of Representatives and the Senate. The Republican Party had long been divided into two camps on immigration issues. One camp focused on the sociocultural aspects of immigration. This camp followed in the nativist tradition of the nineteenth-century anti-immigrant Know-Nothing Party, and favored restrictive policies, especially those that kept out non-Europeans. In the 104th Congress, the nativist tradition was alive and well. Numerous Republicans complained that immigrants who did not learn English and failed to otherwise assimilate would "balkanize" American society (Idelson 1995b:1065).

The other camp in the Republican Party, generally speaking, was driven by economic considerations. It had traditionally supported liberal policies that would provide U.S. businesses with cheap and abundant labor. But by the 1990s this balance between pro-immigration and anti-immigration forces within the Republican Party started to erode. A growing number of Republicans were now casting immigration, especially the economics of immigration, in a different light. Self-identified conservatives espoused anti-government positions that sought to reduce both government services and the taxes used to pay for such services. By the mid-1990s, more and more Republicans saw immigrants as a burden on such public services as schools, hospitals, poor relief, and other benefits. As Lamar Smith (R-TX) put it, "The American people don't want immigrants coming here to live off the taxpayer" (Gimpel and Edwards 1999:213). The Republican Party—now dominated by a large contingent of lawmakers who sought to reduce immigration on economic grounds, cultural grounds, or both—controlled the U.S. legislative process. The party was prepared to push for restrictive measures.

Several individual state governments with relatively high concentrations of immigrants joined the call for more restrictive immigration policies. This was yet another instance where the fractured nature of U.S. political institutions played a critical role. California and other states complained that while payroll taxes went to the federal government, the costs of providing such services as education were borne by the states. California and five other states tried to sue Washington to reimburse them for billions of dollars of services provided to illegal aliens.

In California the success of Proposition 187 had demonstrated that many voters supported denying public services to immigrants. In November 1994 a public referendum on Proposition 187 passed by a margin of 59 percent to 41 percent. Republican Governor Pete Wilson was a strong supporter of the measure, and many believed that his decision to back the proposition was the primary reason for his reelection in 1994 after he had dropped significantly in public opinion polls.

Anti-immigrant groups such as the Federation for American Immigration Reform (FAIR) lobbied in favor of new restrictions. FAIR argued for an immigration moratorium from every conceivable angle, placing particular emphasis on cultural considerations in the mid-1990s. "Suddenly, what used to be their own neighborhood shopping strip, there's not a sign in English," said Daniel Stein, the executive director of FAIR (Idelson 1995b: 1066).

Back in the legislative arena, Lamar Smith (R-TX) and Alan Simpson (R-WY) spearheaded a move for restrictive measures in the 104th Congress (1995–1996). They offered a three-pronged approach that would "get tough" on illegal entries, reduce both illegal and legal immigrants' access to public services, and lower prevailing levels of legal immigration. Smith and Simpson called for increased border patrol and rapid deportations to stem the tide of illegal immigrants. They also proposed restricting legal immigrants' access to public services by denying their claims completely or by combining their income with that of their sponsors in determining their eligibility for means-tested assistance. Moreover, they fought for reductions in legal immigration, hoping to reduce the annual visa quota from 675,000 to 540,000. This included a reduction in employment-based visas from 140,000 to 90,000 per year. The proposal to reduce legal immigration faced considerable opposition. In order to gain passage of such restrictions, Simpson and Smith wanted to keep them bundled together with more popular proposals to fight illegal entries.

Representative Elton Gallegly (R-CA) was tireless in his efforts to prevent immigrants from receiving government services. "If they don't want to pledge their allegiance to the United States, they shouldn't be eligible for food stamps," he contended (Idelson 1995b:1071). Gallegly offered an amendment to Simpson and Smith's bill that would allow states to deny illegal aliens admittance to public schools. In 1982 the Supreme Court had ruled in *Plyler v. Doe* that states could not prohibit undocumented children from attending public schools without congressional authorization. The Gallegly amendment would give states that authorization. This was not a new idea. Jesse Helms (R-NC) had unsuccessfully offered a similar amendment to the IRCA of 1986. But now such a proposal faced better prospects. In addition, Gallegly also recommended denying citizenship to children born in the United States if their parents were illegal aliens.

Ironically, this new push for more restrictive policies took place during a period of prosperity that was in many ways unprecedented in U.S. history. The unemployment rate dropped from 7.4 percent in 1992, to 6.0 percent in 1994, and to 5.4 percent in 1996 (OECD 1999:33). Gross domestic product was increasing at a steady and healthy clip as well, and U.S. growth rates of 5.5 percent in 1992, 5.9 percent in 1994, and 5.4 percent in 1996 were the envy of the industrialized world (U.S. Department of Commerce 1998:148).

In this economic context, employers felt that they needed considerable access to foreign labor. Employers had traditionally counted on considerable support from what was generally a pro-business Republican Party in their efforts to secure access to foreign labor. But now business leaders feared the Republican leadership might enact immigration restrictions, and employer groups quickly mobilized to lobby against such measures. The National Federation of Independent Business railed against the employment eligibility verification system (Gimpel and Edwards 1999:235). Employers in the technology sector such as Microsoft, Intel, Sun Microsystems, Motorola, and Texas Instruments joined together to form an association they called American Business for Legal Immigration (Gimpel and Edwards 1999:243). This group launched a well-funded lobbying effort to prevent immigration restrictions.

Other pro-immigration groups joined the fray. The Council of Jewish Federations opposed proposals to limit refugee admissions, part of the Simpson-Smith bill in the House. Labor unions continued their transition from an anti-immigration to a pro-immigration force, and the AFL-CIO under John Sweeney's leadership lobbied against the bill (Gimpel and Edwards 1999:243–244). The ACLU continued its decades-long battle against an employment eligibility verification system, fearing it would inevitably lead to some form of national identity card (Gimpel and Edwards 1999:235). Hispanic groups such as the National Council of La Raza also opposed identification measures and other proposals that they feared would lead to increased discrimination against people who looked "foreign." The American Immigration Lawyers Association and the CATO Institute, while not enjoying tremendous clout, played critical roles in bringing pro-business Republicans and pro-immigrant Democrats together to oppose the Simpson-Smith plan (Gimpel and Edwards 1999:244, 255).

Many Democrats spoke out against the proposed restrictions. Some argued that to deny benefits to law-abiding immigrants was unjust. "If you are a legal immigrant in this country, you are working here, you are paying taxes, and bad times come to you, you ought to be entitled to everything else that every American is," Representative Jim McDermott (D-WA) told the House (Idelson 1995b:1071). Others contended that there was no need to reduce legal immigration. Representative Howard Berman (D-CA) called legal immigration "healthy and good" (Idelson 1995a:2073).

President Clinton was on record as supporting the Simpson-Smith bill, including some reductions in legal immigration (CQ Almanac 1996:5–3). However, as the legislative process moved on, the administration joined efforts to keep legal and illegal immigration separate (CQ Almanac 1996: 5–3). But when John Huang, a major Democratic fundraiser, conveyed the opposition of Asian Americans to the bill, Clinton became more reserved in his support (Gimpel and Edwards 1999:261). While continuing to back several of the bill's measures, the president spoke out against reductions in legal immigration.

Legislators moved forward on the proposals. Smith and Simpson fought hard to keep their proposals for reductions in legal and illegal immigration intact as a single piece of legislation. Only if they were tied to such popular measures as increased border control, did proposals for decreasing legal immigration stand a chance. The pro-immigration coalition was strong, and Simpson foresaw a defeat for his proposals. Simpson tried to save at least his bill's reductions in legal family-based immigration by placating business interests. "If I take all employment-based provisions out of my bill, will you support it then?" he asked a group of high-tech business executives (Gimpel and Edwards 1999:246). But this offer came too late. The business lobby was unwilling this late in the game to abandon other pro-immigration groups with whom it had been working. The only way to pass any bill was to eliminate all provisions that would reduce legal immigration. In early 1996 an amendment to the bill in the House eliminated the reductions in legal immigration—both employment-based and family-based. Thus, a version of the Simpson-Smith bill (H.R. 2202) that was much more palatable to pro-immigration forces passed the House by a vote of 333 to 87. In the Senate numerous features that pro-immigration groups found objectionable, including the so-called Gallegly amendment, were stripped from the Simpson-Smith bill, and the Senate passed this gutted version of the proposed legislation in May 1996.

Principal differences existed between the two versions of the bill. The Senate bill had neither a Gallegly provision nor a summary exclusion provision, while the House version contained both. Presidential candidate and Kansas Senator Bob Dole favored retaining the Gallegly provision that would deny undocumented children access to public schooling. Dole knew that Clinton would veto such a bill, and he hoped to blame the Democrats afterwards for doing nothing about illegal immigration (CQ Almanac 1996:5–3). In the fall, a conference committee, composed of Republicans only, eliminated the Gallegly amendment to create a compromise bill. Based on Clinton's insistence, the immigration bill was included in a larger omnibus fiscal bill (H.R. 3610), which passed both chambers in late September. It was signed into law by the president on September 30, 1996.

The resulting law increased border control spending and personnel; increased penalties for document fraud; and expedited deportation procedures for illegal aliens. However, nothing was done to halt the employment of undocumented workers, with the insignificant exception of a miniscule, voluntary pilot program for employee verification. While anti-immigration forces proved unable to reduce legal entries, they were able to deny most public benefits, including food stamps and Supplemental Security Income, to legal immigrants as part of sweeping changes made to the U.S. welfare system in 1996, which would dismantle the program known as Aid to Families with Dependent Children.

CONCLUSION

U.S. immigration policies in the 1980s and 1990s highlight both the pluralistic manner in which such policies are made, and the unpredictability of policy outcomes that are produced by such a process. The histories of the IRCA of 1986, the Immigration Act of 1990, and the components of the 1997 omnibus spending resolution that dealt with immigration all demonstrate how complex immigration issues are. Immigration is a multifaceted phenomenon that mobilizes a great number of interests. Organized labor, business, ethnic groups, religious organizations, civil rights groups, immigration lawyers, and other powerful interests influenced the immigration policy-making process in the 1980s and 1990s. U.S. political institutions allowed all of these interests to participate in the decision-making process at various important junctures. In addition, U.S. political institutions fracture the state itself, leading to a dynamic whereby various branches and levels of the governmental apparatus pull immigration policies in different, often contradictory, directions.

One result is that immigration policy outcomes in the United States do not follow economic conditions in a predictable way. Restrictive measures such as the employer sanctions provisions of the 1986 act and the elements of the 1997 omnibus spending resolution that denied benefits to immigrants and expedited their deportation were enacted during periods of relative prosperity. Pluralistic institutional arrangements can also produce policies that are difficult to characterize as either "liberal" or "restrictive." The IRCA of 1986 is perhaps the best example of this in the second half of the twentieth century. The 1986 act offered an amnesty for undocumented workers and greatly increased the number of permits available to temporary workers, while at the same time it placed sanctions on businesses that knowingly hired illegal aliens. Such policies that are not easily fit along a liberal-restrictive continuum are not surprising in this context. U.S. pluralist institutions allow many powerful pro-immigration and anti-immigration forces, both within the state and without, to influence immigration policy. U.S. political institutions provide these forces with numerous points of access from which they can potentially sabotage policy proposals. At times, in order for any policies to get through, numerous competing interests must be appeased simultaneously, and the results are policy outcomes that are both restrictive and liberal.

The 1990s also brought the importance of political institutions to the fore in another way. We have seen in both France and the United States that liberal democratic political institutions often blunt the impact of public opinion on immigration policy outcomes. However, because of the passage of Proposition 187, we can say how institutional arrangements such as a referendum mechanism could in fact translate public opinion into public policy in spite of the opposition of powerful organized interests. Institutional arrangements continued to play a role in California's immigration politics when the U.S. governmental system allowed federal courts to invalidate many aspects of Proposition 187.

III

FRANCE

Chapter 5

Bienvenue

In the wake of the destruction visited upon their country during World War II, the French set about reconstructing much of their national life. Although not without qualification, France's postwar recovery was a remarkable success. The French economy expanded and modernized rapidly, more than at any other time in the country's history. Author Jean Fourastié was inspired to dub these years *"les trente glorieuses,"* or the thirty glorious years, notwithstanding the fact that the expansion's actual duration was somewhat shorter (Fourastié 1979).

During this period, the French state enacted policies designed to recruit large numbers of immigrant workers, at first to spur economic growth and compensate for labor and population shortages engendered by the war, and later to respond to labor needs created by France's expanding economy. In order to compete with other advanced industrialized nations, France adopted aggressive immigrant recruitment policies. The French government sent delegations abroad to locate foreign workers and entice them to immigrate to France. When the state's cumbersome processing of immigrants threatened to slow entries, the government allowed and abetted massive illegal immigration. In the 1960s, the French state signed a slew of labor accords with sending states that promised to supply France with workers in exchange for guarantees concerning safe working and living conditions for immigrants. All in all, French immigrant recruitment was a success. Between 1945 and 1974, France brought in roughly two and one half million immigrant workers who came to settle permanently in France, and an additional one million immigrants who came to reunite with their families (ONI 1974:8).

This confluence of prosperity and liberal entry policies conforms in general to economic explanations for immigration policies. Indeed, the historical record attests to the fact that economic considerations were paramount among state elites' concerns in formulating immigration policies during this period. But this does not mean that France's liberal policies were preordained. In the postwar period, French public opinion was decidedly against immigration (Tapinos 1975:39–41; Wihtol de Wenden 1988:104). Trade unions also opposed immigration, at least most of the time, and repeatedly called for a ban on new entries. From a comparative perspective, we know that the United States maintained discriminatory and restrictive immigration policies during much of this period, even though it, like France, was enjoying economic prosperity (see Chapter 2). This chapter explores how and why France was able to implement liberal immigration policies in the face of opposition from labor unions and the public at large. In light of the dissimilar U.S. case, this chapter tries to determine what it was about France that allowed it to translate its economic good fortune into a policy of recruiting large numbers of immigrant workers.

In this chapter, I emphasize the importance of French political institutions in facilitating immigration policies that seemed correlated with prevailing economic conditions. Immediately after the war, the French state assumed a monopoly over the regulation of immigration, stripping employers of the right they had previously enjoyed to recruit and to select foreign workers largely on their own. The newly created institutional structures, consistent with the country's broader statist arrangements, furnished France with a largely autonomous governmental apparatus that was designed to manage immigration. The state thereafter formulated and implemented immigration policy in an "executive and administrative style" (Wihtol de Wenden 1988:288). After 1945, French immigration laws were not debated in or passed by parliament again until 1980. Rather, the French executive branch made immigration law via administrative memoranda that were not considered in the National Assembly. The memoranda were never even published (Weil 1991:97). Statist institutional arrangements protected political elites from public pressures and encouraged them to make decisions in a technocratic manner. This means that state elites formulated policies they viewed as the proper course of action in light of economic and demographic conditions. For nearly thirty years following World War II, state elites held that the nation's population and manpower shortfalls required policies that encouraged large-scale immigration.

Although relatively autonomous, unitary, and insulated from public opinion, the state did not operate in a political vacuum. The power of business and labor interests placed constraints on the state, and government officials took actions and created institutions that recognized employer and worker clout in this policy area. At first, the state gave employer associations and trade unions formal representation in the National Immigration Office (*Office National d'Immigration*, or ONI). Conflict between the state's so-called social partners led the government to terminate their participation in the ONI, but state elites found it difficult to recruit sufficient numbers of immigrants without employer cooperation. Thus, the state capitulated to employer demands concerning the issuing of work and residency permits. The government thereafter worked closely with employers to bring in millions of immigrant workers. Although trade unions opposed France's liberal immigration policies, business support proved sufficient for the state to implement and maintain policies designed to bring in large numbers of foreign workers.

THE WAR AND ITS AFTERMATH

World War II decimated the French population. During the conflict roughly 600,000 French citizens died, and hundreds of thousands more were seriously injured (Ireland 1994:35; Freeman 1979:69). Moreover, droves of foreign workers fled the country. By 1946, there were an estimated 490,000 fewer foreigners living in France than there had been in 1936 (Tapinos 1975:12). The loss of life, the injuries, and the exodus of foreigners hit the working-age male cohort hardest. In the aftermath of the war, France faced an economic and demographic crisis of historic proportions. Replenishing the nation's population, especially the working population, was one of the most difficult challenges that faced the war-ravaged republic.

French political elites were divided about how immigration policy could best address the nation's population deficit. Two influential camps emerged—one adhering to what was called the "manpower" perspective, the other espousing the "populationist" viewpoint. The manpower school of thought offered a more modest appraisal of France's immigration needs. It held that the state should only recruit immigrants to fill existing job vacancies, and that entries should closely mirror short-term labor demand. Labor leaders generally favored this more limited approach. Ambroise Croizat—general secretary of France's largest labor organization (*Confédération Générale du Travail*, or CGT), deputy in the National Assembly, and leader in the French Communist Party—became labor minister after the war. He strongly advocated the manpower approach to immigration. Many political elites not associated with the labor movement also favored the manpower strategy. For example Jean Monnet, a prominent businessman who had been the primary liaison for arms and financial aid from the United States during the war, and a man who would become one of the principle architects of the European Economic Community, argued that immigration should be closely tied to the labor needs of French industry.

Monnet was appointed head of the Planning Commission (*Commissariat Général du Plan*), a newly created body that was granted the authority to devise what were usually four- or five-year plans for national economic and social priorities. The commission's first such plan called for the importation of 1.5 million foreign workers over a five-year period in light of France's severe labor shortage.

Those who supported the populationist position had more ambitious plans for France's immigration policy. Populationists feared that the losses incurred during the two great wars, the nation's low birthrate, and the graying of the citizenry had led to a demographic crisis that threatened France's position in the world. France needed to repopulate itself if it were to recover from the war and regain its previous stature. Populationists advocated recourse to large-scale immigration as the best method to achieve such repopulation in the short term. Because they wanted to replenish not just the workforce but also the French nation, populationists called for much higher levels of immigration than did those who advocated the manpower position. Charles de Gaulle, head of France's government-in-exile during the war and the country's *de facto* chief executive after the liberation, was the most prominent proponent of the populationist position. Addressing France's Consultative Assembly in March 1945, de Gaulle declared that the population crisis was the "the deepest reason for our misfortune" and the "principal obstacle" to French postwar recovery (Weil 1991:54). Noted demographer Alfred Sauvy argued in favor of the populationist perspective (Sauvy 1946; Debré and Sauvy 1946). Sauvy was appointed director of the newly established National Institute for Population Studies (*Institut National des Études Démographique*, or INED) in October 1945, and he used his position to advance the populationist approach. In one study, Sauvy estimated that France needed to recruit somewhere between 5,290,000 and 14,390,000 immigrants to overcome its labor and population shortage (Sauvy 1946).

In order to replenish the French nation, some populationists supported using a system of ethnic selection to bring in immigrants who would be, in their view, "assimilable." One of the most vocal proponents of this position was Georges Mauco, author of numerous volumes on immigration in the 1930s and 1940s, and secretary general of the High Committee for Population from the end of World War II until 1970. Mauco drew up an ethnic hierarchy of foreigners. The most desirable were "Nordics" (defined as Belgians, Dutch, British, Germans, and others); the next most desirable were the "Mediterraneans" (defined as Spaniards, Portuguese, Italians, and others); and the third most desirable were the "Slavics" (defined as Poles, Czechoslovakians, Yugoslavians, and others) (Weil 1991:56–57). Immigrants from Asia or Africa were deemed undesirable. It should be noted that many who otherwise considered themselves populationists opposed this proposed system of ethnic screening, arguing that it ran contrary to republican values.

The differences between the manpower and populationist camps should not be exaggerated. In practical terms, most political elites, regardless of which argument they were swayed by, were basically on the same page (Tapinos 1975:13). Almost all state elites supported not just liberal immigrant entry laws, but the active recruitment of foreign workers. Almost all elites spoke of the nation's pressing need to bring in millions of immigrants over a relatively short period of time. Few, if any, government officials wanted to retain the employer-run system of immigrant recruitment that had existed before the war. Instead, supporters of both the manpower and the populationist views called for the establishment of a specialized state agency to oversee and administer a recruitment program to bring in millions of foreigners.

THE ESTABLISHMENT OF THE ONI

State elites viewed immigration as a critical component of their plans for postwar recovery, and they were determined to have a government agency regulate the influx of foreigners. Prior to World War II, the French state had not played an extensive role in regulating immigration. For most of the nineteenth century, France had what amounted to open borders. In the 1880s, France started to compel immigrants to register with local authorities once they arrived, but this did not hinder entries. Spontaneous immigration, however, did not satisfy many employers' needs for foreign labor, and in the early twentieth century employers formed organizations to recruit immigrants. The French state granted these employer-controlled agencies—such as the *Comité des Forges* (an association of iron and steel companies), the *Comité des Houillères* (an association of coal-mining companies), and the *Syndicat Agricoles* (an association of agricultural employers)—the authority to recruit and document foreign workers (Singer-Kérel, 1991:283). In 1926, these organizations merged to form the *Société Générale d'Immigration* (SGI). During periods of economic difficulties in the 1920s and 1930s, the state stepped in to restrict immigration by having the Ministry of Labor reject work permit applications and by having the Ministry of Interior deport laborers who did not have valid work permits.

By 1945 state elites were determined to end employer management of immigration and to establish a government agency that would be dedicated to the vital task of regulating immigration. Employers lobbied vigorously against the abolition of the SGI, which had served their foreign labor needs so well in the interwar period (Henneresse 1979:65). Labor leaders, on the other hand, strongly backed the state's position. France's largest trade union association, the *Confédération Générale du Travail* (CGT), abhorred the SGI, claiming that it only looked after employers' interests and never took into consideration the demographic or economic interests of the nation at large (Gani, 1972:29). On November 2, 1945, the French government created the *Office National d'Immigration* (ONI), and granted this agency an administrative monopoly over immigration. The ordinance that created the ONI also dissolved private employer-run organizations that had recruited immigrants before World War II, and it charged the ONI with carrying out policies designed by lawmakers.

The ONI's establishment was indicative of both the French statist tradition that was brought into the area of immigration policy and the neo-corporatist constraints on governmental actions that developed in this sphere. These statist and neo-corporatist dynamics would structure French immigration policy-making in the years to come. By creating the ONI and setting entry policies, state elites formulated unilaterally and unitarily what they believed would be the best approach to immigration. Government officials paid little heed to public opinion, which was decidedly against immigration. There was not much in the way of party competition over these issues, in part because immigration was seen by many in technical and nonpolitical terms. The neo-corporatist constraints were certainly limited. State elites did not try to build consensus by enacting policies that were acceptable to both business and labor interests. Indeed, employers pleaded their case against the ONI to no avail. But at the same time, governmental officials were hesitant to pursue policies that would be opposed by both their social partners. Certainly, we could speculate that the government might have gone ahead with its plans for the ONI regardless of what employers and trade unions thought. But in fact this did not happen. The state had the backing of trade unions on this matter, and a pattern began to form in which the government usually pursued policies that had the support of at least one of the two major class-based interests.

Government elites were sensitive to France's power dynamics in designing the institutional arrangements of the ONI. Clearly, they were aware that the French state was at least somewhat constrained by corporatist power relations. The ONI was to be run by a governing council whose twenty-four seats were divided among representatives from government, business, and organized labor. Also, in an attempt to satisfy adherents to both the manpower and the populationist schools of thought, the ONI was placed under the dual control of the Ministry of Labor, which supported the manpower view, and the Ministry of Population, whose title reflected its perspective. The ONI was intended to regulate many aspects of immigration. Its authority ranged from recruiting immigrants to handling naturalization applications. Employers would now have to submit requests to the ONI for foreign workers, and the newly established agency would in turn recruit immigrants to fill the positions. The ONI also enjoyed considerable financial autonomy because its resources were derived directly from payments made by employers who were supplied with foreign workers via state recruitment programs. The 1945 ordinances setting France's immigration policies rejected the ethnic hierarchy of foreigners championed by Mauco and others. Supporters of discriminatory immigration policies did attempt to facilitate entries from certain ethnic populations by establishing ONI bureaus in some countries and not others, but these tactics proved largely unsuccessful (Weil 1991:62). Without any discriminatory selection criteria, the immigrant population in France became increasingly diverse and non-European in the years that followed.

INITIAL RECRUITMENT EFFORTS

Immediately following the war, the state's immigrant recruitment plan had strong support from organized labor. Organized labor had representatives on the ONI governing council, as well as in the ONI's recruitment office in Italy. Indeed, in the person of Ambroise Croizat, who was the CGT's general secretary and France's minister of labor, the line between government and labor was somewhat obscured on the issue of foreign labor. Croizat asserted that the country needed to import three million immigrant workers to satisfy France's industrial and agricultural labor demand (Gani 1972:28). Other high-ranking CGT officials argued that immigration was a vital necessity for postwar France, and that immigrants added a much-needed young and dynamic component to the workforce (Gani 1972:29–30). It should be noted that not all unions agreed with the CGT. For example, *Force Ouvrière* (FO), a small anti-communist labor confederation, accused the CGT of exploiting the situation for political gains (Wihtol de Wenden 1988:101). But with 5.5 million members, the CGT was by far France's largest labor organization, and with the CGT's backing, it is reasonable to say that the state was supported by the most powerful elements in the labor movement.

Meanwhile, many employers who relied on immigrant labor were unhappy with the new system. Business leaders wanted a freer hand in recruiting foreign workers, such as they had had before the war. Many employers resented having to submit to government oversight of their hiring practices. This limitation was particularly irksome in light of the CGT's influence in the Ministry of Labor and in the ONI's governing council. Certain employers refused to accept workers recruited by the ONI, asserting that the agency had recruited unqualified persons (Garson 1986:6). Business leaders lobbied for the resumption of employer-run recruitment programs like those the SGI had administered. Some employers tried to circumnavigate the ONI by hiring undocumented immigrants. Others avoided the ONI by hiring Algerians, who were granted French citizenship *en masse* in 1947 when France declared that Algeria was no longer a colony but an integral part of the French nation.

This situation in which trade unions supported the state's immigration plans while employers opposed them seemed to turn the politics of immigration upside down. The interests of labor traditionally led trade unions to oppose immigration. For most of the twentieth century labor leaders argued that the influx of immigrant workers reduced wages, undermined the bargaining position of organized labor, and took jobs from French workers. But during a brief interlude after the war, labor leaders not only supported the state's immigration policies, but worked with the government to recruit foreign workers. In 1946, for instance, CGT representatives were part of a French delegation that negotiated a labor accord with Italy, signed in February of that year, which provided for 20,000 Italian miners to come to France (Henneresse 1979:79). Several major factors account for this anomalous behavior by trade unions. The new regime represented a significant improvement over the prewar system from labor's perspective. The establishment of the ONI provided for public control over immigration, rather than leaving employers to their own devices. Immigrant workers coming through these channels would have legal protections unavailable to undocumented workers. And the ONI was to funnel foreign workers away from regions and industries where they might compete with French workers. Perhaps most importantly, labor leaders found it politically expedient to support the state's recruitment program. Parties on the left had done quite well in France's postwar elections, and labor leaders such as Croizat were offered high-level positions. With an opportunity to govern, trade unions (particularly the CGT) were willing to compromise with more mainstream interests.

Nonetheless, trade union support for France's immigrant recruitment plan was short-lived, and the anomalous pro-immigration coalition between the state and labor ended abruptly. The emerging ideological war between capitalism and communism in Europe made it increasingly difficult for trade unions with communist beliefs to work with more mainstream government officials. Ambroise Croizat was forced to resign his post as labor minister in 1947. In response, the CGT took a far more confrontational approach to the government and its immigration policies. As Italian workers entered France without documentation, the CGT accused the government of encouraging illegal immigration so as to provide employers with leverage against trade unions (Gani 1972:47).

Employers, for their part, had traditionally supported immigration. For business leaders, the fact that immigrant workers lowered wages or undermined the negotiating position of organized labor was a positive attribute. Furthermore, in instances of labor shortages foreign workers assumed positions that would otherwise go unfilled. However, although most business leaders supported the state's goal of importing millions of immigrant workers, they opposed how the government planned to accomplish this. Employers did not want to see the ONI manage immigration, and pushed instead for the reestablishment of private immigrant recruitment organizations.

Tensions rose among government, business, and labor leaders, and co-

Table 5.1
Immigration to France, 1946–1955

Year	Legal Immigration	% Change Since 1946
1946	30,171	--
1947	68,223	+126%
1948	57,039	+89%
1949	58,782	+94%
1950	10,525	-65%
1951	20,996	-30%
1952	32,750	+8.5%
1953	15,361	-49%
1954	12,292	-59%
1955	19,029	-37%

Source: OMI 1994

operation within the ONI's tripartite governing council became almost impossible. On September 20, 1948, the French state terminated employer and trade union representation in the ONI by decree (Henneresse 1979: 83). The CGT responded by reversing its position on immigration policy. At its National Congress in October, the CGT drafted a resolution that read: "The Congress . . . pronounces itself against all new entries of foreign labor" (CGT 1948:274). From this point on, the CGT refused to participate in immigrant recruitment programs. Other unions joined the fray. The *Confédération Française des Travailleurs Chrétiens* (CFTC), a sizeable Catholic labor organization, also demanded at its 1948 Congress that immigration be brought to a halt (Gani 1972:50).

Meanwhile, the French state was having severe difficulties bringing in foreign workers. For example, the February 1946 accord with Italy provided for 20,000 Italian workers to come to France, but after nine months only 3,000 had actually arrived (Tapinos 1975:28). French and Italian authorities tackled the question anew by signing a second accord in November 1946 that envisioned 200,000 Italian immigrants settling in France in 1947, but in the end only 51,000 came (Tapinos 1975:28). To put this fact in perspective, we should recall that even the most modest of the recruitment plans, the Monnet Plan, called for the importation of 300,000 immigrants per year. But only approximately 68,000 non-seasonal immigrants came to France in 1947, and approximately 10,000 fewer than that came in each of the next two years (see Table 5.1). Indeed, it took the ONI an entire

Table 5.2
ONI Fulfillment of Employer Requests for Immigrant Workers,
1947–1948

ECONOMIC SECTOR	REQUESTS FULFILLED
Agriculture and Forestry	23.2%
Mining	47.2%
Metallurgic Industries	90.0%
Construction	37.5%
Domestic Service	87.8%
Other	62.4%
TOTAL	46.5%

Source: Henneresse 1979:74

decade to bring a total of 325,168 permanent settlers to France. The permanent migration of some 177,000 Algerian workers (who were French citizens) between 1946 and 1955 augmented the labor influx, but hardly made up for the shortfall (Tapinos 1975:29–34).

There were numerous obstacles to immigration. For one thing, there was competition for labor, as other nations such as Belgium and Switzerland turned to immigration to supplement their workforces during this period. France also suffered from a housing shortage—certainly a detriment to recruiting new residents. Another difficulty was the halting progress of France's postwar economic recovery. Between 1945 and 1949, the government was forced to devaluate the French *franc* on four separate occasions. France furthermore went through recessions in 1949–1950 and in 1952–1953. This somewhat dampened the desire of state elites and employers to bring in additional labor. It also made France less attractive to potential immigrants. In 1949, the ONI's director Pierre Bideberry claimed that the country's low levels of immigration were a reflection of the fact that French employers had all the workers they needed (Henneresse 1979:71).

However, the primary reasons behind France's low levels of immigration rested with the ONI's slow-moving bureaucracy. Unable to efficiently process immigrant entries, the ONI created bottlenecks in the influx of immigrant workers. Contrary to Bideberry's claims, many enterprises lacked workers and turned to the agency in an attempt to satisfy their need for immigrant labor. But the ONI proved remarkably unable to handle employers' requests for immigrant workers in an efficient manner. In 1947–1948 the ONI fulfilled less that half of employers' requests for foreign workers (see Table 5.2). The ONI's failure was particularly pronounced in the area of agriculture, where only a quarter of the requests were satisfied; and in construction, where roughly two-thirds of all requests went unfulfilled. These numbers may only be the tip of the iceberg, for it is unknown how many requests were not submitted in anticipation of ONI failure.

For most of the first decade after the war, the French government tried to facilitate massive immigration in light of what state elites believed were clear economic and demographic imperatives. After the state terminated tripartite representation in the ONI, it tried to attain its immigration goals largely on its own. The December 1948 decree that ended employer and trade union representation in the ONI also placed a renewed emphasis on family immigration in an attempt to bolster the influx. In July 1950, a new ONI recruitment mission was established in Gemersheim, West Germany. The French state, in March 1951, signed yet another labor agreement with Italy. In March 1954, France signed its first labor accord with Greece. But operating in a mostly unilateral manner, the state fell far short of its immigration goals, as the ONI proved inadequate to the task of importing hundreds of thousands of immigrant workers each year. To rectify matters, the French state would soon change its approach to immigration. In the years to come, the government would work very closely with business interests, setting out on a course that would help promote a massive influx of immigrants.

LAISSEZ-FAIRE IMMIGRATION POLICIES

In the mid-1950s, French government officials, distressed by the nation's failure to replenish its population and labor force, renewed their commitment to massive immigration, and searched for new strategies to bring it about. In its 1953 economic blueprint for the country, the *Commissariat Général du Plan* stressed that immigrant recruitment should not be based on short-term needs, and that high levels of immigration were indispensable to the country's economic goals. But in light of its failures, it was unclear exactly how the state could facilitate immigration. What was clear was that state elites had no intention of limiting immigration as trade unions demanded. Rather, they felt that the nation desperately needed voluminous infusions of foreign labor. In order to facilitate such infusions, the government would need to work closely with French employers.

Of all the obstacles to large-scale immigration, none presented more of an impediment than the bottlenecks created by the ONI's processing of foreign workers. Business leaders abhorred the agency. Even when employers did try to recruit immigrants through its offices, the ONI could not satisfy more than half of their requests. Furthermore, it was unknown how many employers needed workers but did not bother submitting requests that as often as not went unfulfilled. The solution most preferred by employers was to allow foreign workers to bypass ONI procedures for entering the country, a tactic that would certainly eliminate the bottlenecks.

Eager to increase immigration, government elites decided on a strategy that relied on the "regularization" of immigrants. Undocumented immigrants were allowed, even encouraged, to bypass the ONI and to enter the country illegally. Once these foreigners had found lodging and employment, the state provided them with work and residency permits. These documents legalized or "regularized" an immigrant's status, providing her or him with a sort of preplanned amnesty. The requirement that would-be immigrants procure work and residency permits from the ONI before coming to France had been at the heart of the bottlenecks. By regularizing immigrants after their arrival, delays were avoided.

France had regularized undocumented immigrants before, but only on a limited basis. Immediately after the war, the French government allowed a small number of Italian workers to bypass ONI procedures by letting them enter the country, and then regularizing their status. In 1949, the state, via a circular issued from the Ministry of Labor, declared that all nationals, not just Italians, were eligible for regularization. In practice, however, very few illegal immigrants were regularized. French officials wanted to maintain their authority over the nation's borders, and administrators had hoped that the ONI could funnel immigrant workers into the geographic regions and industrial sectors that needed them most. For these reasons, the government required most immigrants to be processed by the ONI.

But by the mid-1950s, state elites began to believe that the benefits of massive immigration spurred by regularizations would outweigh the costs associated with eroding the state's control over its borders. The desire of state elites to facilitate massive immigration was heightened by France's rapidly improving economic prospects. Moreover, the colonial war in Algeria forced the state to call reserves and to extend military service, thus depleting the country's indigenous labor supply even further. The conflict also dampened Algerian immigration, which had become quite important to the French labor market. From 1954 to 1962, Algerian immigration to France averaged a relatively low 11,000 persons per year (Tapinos 1975: 49). At the same time, West Germany was experiencing its "economic miracle," which drove its labor demand up sharply, adding yet another competitor into the market for immigrant workers.

French employers, for their part, were in dire need of additional workers. The economic upswing of 1955–1956 exacerbated labor shortages. France's largest employers' association, the *Confédération National du Patronat Français* (CNPF), lobbied the government to remove obstacles to immigration (Garson 1986:7). Immigration emerged as a top priority for French business. In 1956, Georges Villiers, the president of the CNPF, told his organization's general assembly that foreign labor was "indispensable" to the nation's economy (Henneresse 1979:125). The CNPF held that it would be "impossible not to resort to [immigration] in very large proportions" (CNPF 1956:101).

State elites decided that they had no choice but to allow foreign workers to enter the country outside the auspices of the ONI and to regularize their status afterwards. The French executive branch made this decision in an administrative manner without any legislative action. On April 18, 1956, the minister of labor, Jean Minjoz, issued a circular that instructed administrators to accept all regularization requests in cases where the lack of manpower risked slowing economic growth, and to issue temporary work permits to foreigners waiting for their regularization requests to be approved. In effect, this circular put the regularization procedure on a par with immigration that went through ONI channels. The French state would still have authority in the matter of who resided and worked in France, but the documentation procedures became more of a rubber stamp than a process that regulated entry. From then on, almost all applicants would be regularized, a move that was intended to encourage large-scale "clandestine" immigration.

In the years between the termination of tripartite representation in the ONI and the adoption of regularization as a systematic method for large-scale immigrant recruitment, the French state had for the most part formulated and implemented its immigration policies without the support or participation of its so-called social partners. In light of state failures, and in response to employer pressure, public officials embraced regularizations. By 1956, France's largest employer association, the CNPF, could declare, "We have, on this point, attracted the government's attention. They share our sentiments" (CNPF, 1956:101).

Because immigrants could now bypass the ONI and go directly to employers, businesses had what amounted to a free hand in hiring foreigners. Businesses could select their own workers rather than accept those chosen by the ONI. By hiring foreign workers themselves, businesses also avoided ONI processing fees. Thus, business organizations such as the Paris Chamber of Commerce applauded the move, stating, "The Government seems to have realized the necessity not only of not impeding foreign workers' entry into France, nor only of letting it operate naturally, but of aiding the movement" (CCIP, 1957:244).

France's corporatist constraints, as we have noted, were not such that they required consensus among all three groups. In fact, trade unions were vehemently opposed to the 1956 circular, for it amounted to a *laissez-faire* immigration policy. But under the statist-corporatist dynamics of French immigration policy, the government seemed to need support from only one of its two social partners for the successful formulation and implementation of its immigration policies. With state officials and business leaders firmly behind the move to a *laissez-faire* entry policy, labor's objections fell on deaf ears. Although business leaders no longer had formal access to immigration lawmaking, their informal influence perpetuated certain corporatist institutional dynamics.

The Minjoz circular of 1956 was implemented immediately and effec-

Table 5.3
Immigrants Regularized in France, 1955–1964

Year	Immigrants Regularized	% Change Since 1955
1955	5,695	--
1956	18,229	+220%
1957	56,131	+886%
1958	37,624	+561%
1959	23,000	+304%
1960	28,814	+406%
1961	41,874	+635%
1962	60,470	+962%
1963	75,841	+1,232%
1964	109,542	+1,823%

Source: Garson 1985

tively. The number of foreigners who were regularized increased tenfold, jumping from 5,695 in 1955 to 56,131 in 1957 (see Table 5.3). France's recourse to regularizations spurred overall migration to its highest levels in the postwar era to that point. Between 1955 and 1957 total immigration to France rose almost sixfold, climbing from 19,029 to 111,693 (see Table 5.4). Employers' claims that bottlenecks created by the ONI had been the primary drag on immigration to France seemed to be borne out.

State elites were taken aback by the policy's success. Alarmed by the sharp increase in illegal entries, the government moved to reintroduce certain restrictions. By 1960 the number of annual regularizations had been reduced to roughly 28,000. This brought the total number of entries to less than 50,000. Both these numbers were higher than they had been before the 1956 circular, but they fell short of state and employer targets. A state-sponsored report criticized the government's reticence to encourage clandestine immigration (Henneresse 1979:161–162). By the early 1960s, government leaders concluded that they had no choice but to forgo almost all restrictions on immigrant entries. As Minister of State Jean-Marcel Jeanneney put it, "if we held to the strict application of regulations and international accords, we might lack the manpower we need" (Garson 1986:5). Circulars issued by the Ministry of Labor in February 1962 and March 1964 allowed for even greater recourse to clandestine immigration. As a result, the influx of undocumented workers rose dramatically. In 1965 more than 120,000 foreign workers came to France outside the auspices of

Table 5.4
Immigration to France, 1955–1964

Year	Legal Immigration	% Change Since 1955
1955	19,029	--
1956	65,428	+244%
1957	111,693	+487%
1958	82,818	+335%
1959	44,179	+132%
1960	48,914	+157%
1961	78,927	+315%
1962	113,069	+494%
1963	115,523	+507%
1964	154,731	+713%

Source: OMI 1994

the ONI, and they were subsequently regularized. This represented almost 80 percent of all foreign workers introduced into the French labor market that year. French immigration had clearly become dependent on clandestine entries.

RECRUITING IMMIGRANTS

France's recourse to spontaneous entries, more than any other policy initiative, brought about large-scale immigration. But regularizations were not the only political development driving the influx. State and business leaders also worked together to establish and run labor recruitment programs abroad. For example, officials from France's largest construction industry association, the *Fédération Nationale du Bâtiment* (FNB), and the ONI went to Italy to study additional measures to increase immigration. They concluded that training programs were necessary to improve the skill levels of would-be immigrants, and the Italian government quickly established such a program based on the FNB-ONI recommendations (Henneresse 1979:129). Another delegation of state and employer representatives conducted an extensive immigrant recruitment campaign between 1956 and 1958 in Sicily and Sardinia to find foreign workers for the coal-mining industry (Henneresse 1979:128).

When the metallurgic industries found in the early 1960s that they needed even greater supplies of immigrant workers than they had in the past, the Ministry of Labor authorized the UIMM (the sector's largest employers' association) to send representatives abroad in search of laborers (Henneresse 1979:135). The UIMM discovered that Spain had extensive pools of trained workers, and the ONI followed up on this report by launching a program to recruit Spanish immigrants (Henneresse 1979:135). Meanwhile, when the automobile producer Citroën needed additional workers, the ONI had the company send its own representatives to Athens to find laborers. Once there, Citroën administered medical examinations and qualification tests on behalf of the French Republic, and those who passed were allowed by the ONI to come to France and work for Citroën (Henneresse 1979:138).

The French state also launched a diplomatic initiative to secure foreign labor. With immigrant workers in such great demand, sending nations were able to win concessions for their nationals, usually in the form of improved working and living conditions. These concessions were made by instrument of international treaties. Receiving nations such as France were more than willing to sign such accords in the 1960s in return for guaranteed access to the sending nations' labor markets. Competing with such countries as West Germany and Switzerland, France signed immigration accords at a frenzied pace. In succession, the French government signed agreements with Morocco (June 1, 1963), Tunisia (August 9, 1963), Portugal (December 31, 1963), Yugoslavia (January 25, 1965), and Turkey (April 8, 1965). At the insistence of French negotiators, the Evian accords that ended the war with Algeria allowed free circulation between the two countries for French and Algerian nationals. The primary objective of this clause was to allow those who supported France during the war to leave Algeria if they wished. But it also allowed Algerians to migrate to France with few restrictions.

CONCLUSION

By the 1970s France had become one of the world's leading importers of foreign labor. The route had certainly been circuitous, but the French state managed nonetheless to facilitate the kind of immigrant influx that elites had almost unanimously called for immediately after World War II, and that analysts in hindsight deemed indispensable to the remarkable economic recovery enjoyed by France and other industrialized nations of western Europe. Because public officials rejected proposals to select immigrants on the basis of ethnicity, France developed significant minority populations during the postwar boom, and the country was transformed into a more multicultural community. As we will see in the next two chapters, this development would influence the politics of immigration in France for years to come.

During the postwar era, France developed statist institutions for formulating and implementing its immigration policies. As we have seen, the type of legislative debates over immigration that might have politicized these issues were never held. Immigration was decidedly not a policy that engendered much party competition either in the National Assembly or in electoral campaigns. Instead, the French executive made myriad decisions—to establish a state monopoly over immigration, to recruit massive numbers of immigrants, to condone and even encourage illegal immigration, to establish programs to find and recruit foreign workers, and to sign labor accords with sending states—in an administrative manner. State elites viewed immigration policies as a predominantly technical economic undertaking, and thus formulated and implemented policies that they believed were dictated by prevailing economic conditions.

That said, we have also seen that the state did not go it alone completely. Public officials were cognizant of the power of business and labor. This was first evident in the original tripartite design of the ONI. But the state did not need the support of both business and labor. By the mid-1950s, state and business elites were working closely together to recruit large numbers of immigrant workers, much to the dismay of trade union leaders. At the urging of business representatives, the state allowed undocumented immigrants to enter France undeterred, freeing employers to hire foreigners as they pleased. Afterwards, the state readily provided these foreign workers with the permits necessary to legalize their status, in what amounted to a preplanned, systematic amnesty. When the influx of immigrants, a majority of whom were undocumented, still proved inadequate for French industrial needs, the state sent recruitment delegations consisting of government and employer representatives abroad to search for additional labor. In some instances, the state allowed businesses to conduct their own recruitment in foreign countries. In the end, a largely informal coalition between the state and employers was the driving force behind France's liberal immigration policies that facilitated the arrival of millions of foreigners during the postwar economic boom.

Chapter 6

French Immigration Policies in Hard Times

In the 1970s France's rapid postwar expansion, the so-called *trente glorieuses*, came to an abrupt halt, and the country experienced a severe economic crisis. There were indications of a slowdown as early as 1966–1967, when the French economy went into a mild recession. But the economic difficulties of the 1970s proved to be worse than most people had expected. At the outset of the decade, the global deceleration of growth became a full-scale world economic crisis when several oil-producing nations raised petroleum prices dramatically. Inflation and unemployment rose; domestic production and equities markets fell. In direct response to these developments, the French government decided to suspend immigration. The government moved to prevent the arrival of foreign workers and their families who wanted to settle permanently in France. In addition, the government enacted new measures to fight clandestine immigration and to crack down on black-market jobs that employed many immigrants, particularly illegal aliens. Although it was presented as a temporary measure in the summer of 1974, the so-called immigration ban was extended in the fall of that year, and it has been in effect ever since.

France's decision to restrict immigration seemed a logical, almost inevitable, response to the economic crisis of the 1970s and the high levels of unemployment it engendered. In many respects, this is an excellent example of economic conditions determining immigration policy outcomes, with economic difficulties leading to restrictive measures. This chapter explores why economic hardships resulted in the French immigration ban. Social scientists are often fascinated with "counterintuitive" outcomes, and this is understandable. We are struck by the unexpected, for it presents us with puzzles to solve. But this fascination runs the risk of blinding us about why we sometimes get the outcomes we expect.

In order to understand how French immigration policy was made during this period, we would be well advised to retain a certain level of contingency in our analysis. Indeed, there are compelling reasons to doubt the inevitability of France's immigration policy outcomes. From a comparative perspective, we know that the United States faced similar economic difficulties during this same period. Yet the U.S. refrained from imposing immigration restrictions, actually allowing the number of entries to increase over the course of the 1970s (see Chapter 3). Furthermore, if we move beyond a cursory examination of the historical narrative, we discover that French public officials abandoned their initial attempts to restrict immigration in 1972–1973. The failure of French state elites to implement and maintain these earlier restrictions indicates that immigration policy outcomes were more contingent than one might think.

This chapter suggests that French institutional arrangements played a critical role in translating the country's economic difficulties into restrictive immigration policies. Statist institutional structures furnished France with a largely autonomous governmental apparatus that made immigration policy decisions in an "executive and administrative style" (Wihtol de Wenden 1988:288). None of the restrictive measures enacted during the 1970s was an act of parliament. Instead, the French executive branch "issued" these policies via decrees and circulars that were never considered in the National Assembly. In fact, these administrative memoranda that set French immigration policy were never even published (Weil 1991:97). Statist institutions insulated political elites from public pressures and encouraged them to make decisions in a technocratic manner. State elites at the time viewed labor migration as a predominantly economic issue that needed to be managed. In light of France's economic difficulties of the 1970s, public officials were convinced that restrictive immigration policies were in order. Immigrant housing shortages and rising racial tensions reinforced this belief. The French Council of Ministers, unencumbered by separation of powers or even parliamentary debate, therefore placed restrictions on immigrant entries as it saw fit.

The French state's autonomy was not without qualification. French institutional arrangements also empowered business and labor interests, and the influence of these interests placed some constraints on state action. While the French government in the second half of the twentieth century often formulated immigration policies unilaterally, the historical record also indicates that the state was often hesitant to implement immigration policies that did not have the backing of at least one of its two so-called social partners, that is, business and labor. This chapter demonstrates how these corporatist constraints led the government to rescind restrictive measures in 1972–1973. Ironically, these corporatist constraints usually put the state in a strategically advantageous position. Employers had a strong tendency to back liberal policies, while trade unions usually preferred restrictive policies. Thus, it seemed that the state would have the support of at least one of its social partners for whichever avenue it chose. When the state moved to restrict immigration in 1974, it did so with the support of France's labor movement, and over the objections of business leaders.

THE BURDENS OF SUCCESS

France's efforts to recruit foreign workers from the end of World War II until the early 1970s were quite successful. The number of immigrant workers and their family members who came each year to settle permanently in France had climbed from roughly 73,000 in 1947 to about 255,000 in 1970 (OMI 1994). Over the same period of time, the foreign population residing in France rose from 1 to 3 million. Many economists believed that immigrant labor was indispensable to the postwar economic recovery enjoyed by France and by the rest of western Europe (Kindleberger 1967).

France's success at recruiting massive numbers of immigrants during the postwar expansion also presented the country with a series of problems it had failed to anticipate adequately. One of the most pressing domestic problems facing France in the 1950s and 1960s was a shortage of adequate housing for the working class in general, and for immigrant workers in particular. By 1968 over a quarter of the entire French population was living in overcrowded conditions (Minces 1973:372). Within the context of this general housing shortage, immigrants found themselves especially disadvantaged. For one thing, foreigners often did not know how to find residences in France, and they were unaware of their rights regarding housing in many instances (Minces 1973:370; Calame and Calame 1972:152). More perniciously, many landlords distrusted immigrants because of their racial or ethnic backgrounds, and as a result foreigners had to pay higher rents than did French nationals for the same housing (Calame and Calame 1972:153–154). Official policies discriminated against immigrants as well. French citizens were given priority over immigrants in the allocation of state-subsidized housing, and limits were placed on the number of foreign families allowed to reside in state-supported apartment buildings called *Habitation à Loyer Modéré*, or HLM.

With so few housing opportunities, some immigrant workers resorted to constructing their own makeshift housing. Shantytowns, known in France as *bidonvilles*, sprang up in urban areas. Urban renovation programs of the 1950s and 1960s pushed foreign workers out of city centers and toward the urban periphery where immigrants built most of their *bidonvilles*. By the late 1960s over 75,000 people lived in these shantytowns (Calame and

Calame 1972:173). The French media provided extensive coverage of the *bidonvilles*, and the emergence of "third-world" conditions on French soil became a public scandal.

As public criticism mounted, President Georges Pompidou and Prime Minister Jacques Chaban-Delmas decided to demolish the immigrant shantytowns. Although French law required the state to provide replacement housing for anyone it displaced, Housing Secretary André Vivien remarked that "these two operations need not occur simultaneously" (*Le Monde*, August 23–24, 1970). The Pompidou government decided to eradicate the *bidonvilles* immediately and worry about providing alternative housing afterwards. The newly homeless foreigners protested their evictions, which led to confrontations with the French police (Ireland 1994:41–42; Miller 1981:85). In spite of these immigrant demonstrations, the government continued to eradicate the shantytowns, and by 1973 most of the *bidonvilles* were things of the past.

While the government failed to provide sufficient replacement housing for former shantytown dwellers, it did make some effort to ameliorate immigrant housing conditions. In the 1960s, the government steadily increased the budget for the Social Action Fund (*Fonds d'Action Sociale*, or FAS) which subsidized housing projects, including several that were designed to house immigrants displaced by the demolition of the *bidonvilles*. Between 1966 and 1968, HLM programs provided 5,000 replacement residences for foreigners who had lived in the shantytowns (Calame and Calame 1972:169). Between 1970 and 1973, the Pompidou government increased the total budget for immigrant housing sixfold, hiking state spending in this area from 25 to 150 million *francs* (Minces 1973:375). Yet these provisions fell far short of the need, and many immigrants remained homeless or found themselves in dangerous and insalubrious accommodations.

Another serious problem facing France by the early 1970s was mounting hostility toward immigrants. Throughout the country, foreigners, especially North Africans, were the victims of violent attacks. In 1971 French fascists killed North African workers in random attacks in the Midi region (Miller 1981:97). Later that year a Frenchman shot dead a 16-year-old Algerian boy named Djellali Ben Ali (Benoît 1980:273–274). When anti-racist demonstrations were held in Djellali's neighborhood, a massive contingent of police was deployed. The incident galvanized parts of the French intelligentsia. Public figures such as Jean-Paul Sartre, Jean Genet, and Michel Foucault denounced both racist attacks and the extensive police presence in immigrant neighborhoods. In 1972 an officer shot dead a North African immigrant named Mohamed Diab in the Versailles police station. A silent rally held to protest Diab's murder was broken up violently by the police. The police officer who shot Diab never went to jail. The following year, tensions rose in Marseilles after a mentally ill Algerian killed a French bus

driver. During August and September, fifteen North Africans were mur-
dered in the Marseilles area, apparently in reprisal.

Xenophobes in France organized anti-immigrant associations. One neo-
fascist group called New Order led public rallies and instigated violent
confrontations with foreigners. In the wake of the French bus driver's
death, another anti-immigrant group called the Marseilles Defense Committee (*Comité de défense de Marseilles*) was formed. These groups did not
have the widespread support that the National Front would enjoy in the
1980s and 1990s. Nonetheless, the activities of New Order, the Marseilles
Defense Committee, and others were indicative of the rising social tensions
in France in the late 1960s and early 1970s. The attacks against immigrants
were not discrete events. Rather, they were part of a general trend of increasing hostility toward foreign workers. Immigrants at one march held a
banner that read: "Djellali, Diab, Marseilles, how far, how long?" (*Le
Monde*, December 19, 1973).

It was more difficult for the French state to address these racial and
ethnic tensions than it was to address the housing issue. The homeless, after
all, could be housed provided the necessary financial resources were available. Although they were clearly disconcerted by the rising tide of hate in
the country, French leaders limited themselves to largely symbolic gestures
to combat anti-immigrant sentiments. In July 1972 the government passed
a law that officially condemned racism. In 1973 President Georges Pompidou declared that France was profoundly anti-racist. (Wihtol de Wenden
1988:161–162). A general consensus emerged among political elites that
the best way to combat racism was to integrate the foreign population, but
most officials were at a loss as to how such integration might be accomplished.

State officials were obviously concerned with the socioeconomic problems facing France's growing immigrant population in the late 1960s and
early 1970s. Many in government believed that issues of immigrant entries
and immigrant incorporation were interrelated. In a report to the Economic
and Social Council, Corentin Calvez suggested that reducing immigration
would ameliorate the housing crisis (Calvez 1969:312). Pompidou stated
that decreasing immigrant entries would help lower racial and ethnic tensions (Wihtol de Wenden 1988:161–162).

But in the end, the French government did not alter its entry policies in
response to the housing shortage or social tensions. Instead, the state's
policy responses to problems of immigrant incorporation were compart-
mentalized. The state devised new housing policies to tackle the immigrant
housing crisis. Racist attacks were usually dealt with on a case-by-case
basis. When racism was addressed in general terms, the state offered gestures of condemnation, and little more. Regardless of the numerous incorporation problems that arose from the late 1940s until the early 1970s, the
state continued to recruit immigrants to satisfy the nation's labor needs.

THE RECESSION OF 1966–1967

While numerous state elites saw the immigrant housing shortage, rising social tensions, and other problems associated with integrating foreign workers into French society as reasons to limit immigration, it was only when economic difficulties threatened to reduce demand for foreign labor that France actually placed restrictions on immigrant entries. The first signs that France's remarkable postwar growth was slowing down came in 1966–1967 when the country experienced a short recession. France's economic expansion relented, producing a slowdown in hiring nationwide. The government responded by placing new restrictions on clandestine immigration. In 1968 the Ministry of Social Affairs issued a circular that curtailed regularizations for unskilled workers. Exceptions were made for Portuguese migrants, skilled workers, and immigrants employed in domestic service. Nonetheless, the new restrictions had a noticeable impact. The percentage of immigration accomplished through regularization dropped from 76 percent in 1968 to 61 percent in 1970 (Wihtol de Wenden 1988:150). This represented the reversal of a steep upward trend in regularizations. Fewer regularizations meant fewer immigrants. The total number of immigrant workers coming to France, excluding seasonal workers, fell by 13 percent between 1967 and 1968 (ONI 1974:8).

Government elites began to doubt the prudence of continued large-scale immigration in the wake of the 1966–1967 recession. Political leaders came to realize that postwar economic growth would not last forever, and they began to plan accordingly. The government initiated a reexamination of its immigration policy under the auspices of the Economic and Social Council in 1968. In a report commissioned by the Council, Corentin Calvez claimed that exuberant immigrant recruitment had led to an enormous influx of foreign workers that would soon far exceed France's labor needs (Calvez 1969). Calvez recommended that France limit immigration, and in recognition of France's statist-corporatist arrangements he concluded it was "necessary to involve . . . representatives of employer and worker organizations" in the formulation and implementation of immigration policy (Calvez 1969:316).

The Economic and Social Council's deliberations foreshadowed the politics of immigration restrictions that would unfold a few years later. Trade union elites had long called for significant reductions in labor migration to France. Thus it came as no surprise when every delegate from France's largest trade organizations—the *Confédération Générale du Travail* (CGT), the *Confédération Française Démocratique du Travail* (CFDT), and *Force Ouvrière* (FO)—voted in favor of a resolution calling for a more restrictive entry policy. State elites had supported liberal immigration policies for over two decades. But on the Council they reversed their position and voted for restrictions in light of what they perceived to be changing economic conditions. Employer representatives maintained their traditional pro-immigration positions and opposed Calvez's recommendations. When the issue came to a vote, business delegates abstained. Nonetheless, the coalition between state and trade union officials was sufficient to carry the day, and the Council issued its own statement endorsing Calvez's call for greater immigration restrictions (JO 1969). The Council's recommendations were non-binding, but they were indicative of things to come.

The downturn in the economy was short-lived. France's economy rebounded quickly and vigorously as the 1960s came to a close. In 1969, French industrial production was 10 percent higher than it had been the previous year (IMF 1998:16). Labor demand remained high as the unemployment rate fell from 1.9 percent in 1968 to 1.7 percent in 1970 (OECD 1984:476). Employers found it relatively easy to circumnavigate the 1968 restrictions on illegal immigration. French employers reclassified job vacancies so that they fit the categories of skilled positions deemed eligible for regularization (Moulier and Tapinos 1979:135–136). Faced with a tight labor market, French public officials did little to discourage this practice. Overall, France allowed the influx of legal immigrant workers to rise from 93,165 in 1968 to 174,243 in 1970, while the number of immigrants settling permanently in France for purposes of family reunification was allowed to climb from 55,812 to 80,952 over the same period (ONI 1974: 8).

THE MARCELLIN-FONTANET CIRCULARS

Part of France's statist tradition involved the development and implementation of economic plans, usually four or five years in duration, that were designed to build policy programs that were the result of rational economic analysis, rather than interest group lobbying. Mark Kesselman suggests that "planning was so successful in part because it *excluded* many groups" (Kesselman et al. 1997:161, emphasis in original). Although the 1966–1967 recession had passed quickly, the 1970s brought economic uncertainty to advanced industrialized nations. The agency charged with formulating France's economic blueprint, the *Commissariat Général du Plan*, estimated that sectors relying heavily on foreign workers, such as construction, would experience low levels of economic growth in the period from 1971 to 1975 (*Commissariat Général du Plan* 1971). The agency warned that uncontrolled immigration could hurt French workers in a great many sectors. The plan thus called for a decrease in the number of immigrant entries to 75,000 per year—a reduction of over 50 percent. The *Commissariat* urged France to exercise greater control over the employment of clandestine immigrants and reduce the number of regularizations. The *Commissariat Général du Plan*, like the Social and Economic Council, recognized that the state faced certain neo-corporatist constraints on its actions in the area of immigration policy. The agency thus concluded that the "implementation of these multiple and complex measures require . . . supervision by trade unions and employer organizations" (*Commissariat Général du Plan* 1971:87).

In 1972 the government of Georges Pompidou set out to restrict clandestine immigration by instrument of two administrative memoranda, one issued by the minister of interior, Raymond Marcellin, and the other issued by the minister of labor, Joseph Fontanet. These memoranda, collectively known as the Marcellin-Fontanet circulars, aimed to curtail illegal immigration by changing France's laws concerning the granting of residency and work permits. Specifically, the Marcellin-Fontanet circulars sought to end the decades-old practice of "regularization" by which undocumented immigrants came to France, found employment, and then received the necessary paperwork—in that order and without many obstacles. State and business elites had facilitated the regularization process for over two decades in order to increase international labor migration to France. But in the early 1970s state elites saw the elimination of this practice as a logical place to begin limiting the migratory influx.

Prior to the Marcellin-Fontanet circulars, an illegal immigrant who sought the permits necessary to regularize his or her status only needed to provide the state with a written job offer. Under the new regulations, an employer who wanted to hire an undocumented immigrant had to ask the National Employment Agency (*Agence Nationale de l'Emploi*, or ANE) for the necessary permits. The ANE was required to search for a French national or a legal immigrant to fill the position. If the ANE found someone for the job, the employer's request was denied. If the ANE was not able to find someone, the departmental labor director could reject the request on the grounds that there were already too many foreign workers in that particular economic sector. The department's prefect (chief executive officer) could veto the request as well for other reasons, such as an employer's failure to provide housing for the worker. If at any stage the immigrant's request for regularization were denied, he or she would be expelled from France. The Marcellin-Fontanet circulars provided no legal recourse for unsuccessful applicants. All in all, the new policies erected a formidable matrix of obstacles for any immigrants who sought residency and work permits.

Most French employers wanted to see no such restrictions. France's largest employer organization, the *Conseil National du Patronat Français*, asserted in 1972 that the "role of foreign labor in industrial development is of absolute importance" (*Économie Géographie* 1972:9). The CNPF claimed that industrial nations would suffer a labor shortage of roughly 11 million workers over the following ten years, while nations of emigration would only have a labor surplus of between 7.8 and 10.4 million workers, thus producing a global shortage of immigrants (*Notes et*

Arguments 1972:1). Clearly, in the eyes of business leaders, this was hardly the time for immigration restrictions. Employers wanted to establish additional accords with sending nations and to increase the number of recruitment missions (*Notes et Arguments* 1972:7). Employers also favored continued reliance on regularization because it allowed businesses "to respond to urgent needs and to choose workers for themselves" (Weil 1991: 73).

Business leaders complained that the Marcellin-Fontanet circulars complicated and slowed the recruitment of foreign workers at a time when their labor was still needed. The construction industry, with its heavy reliance on immigrant laborers, voiced perhaps the most vigorous opposition to the new measures. The Parisian Construction Federation (*Fédération Parisien de Batiment*, or FPB) sent questionnaires about the circulars to employers and forwarded the responses to the government. The results of the survey attested to the difficulties employers experienced as a consequence of the Marcellin-Fontanet policy. The president of the FPB also wrote a letter to the Ministry of Social Affairs in which he complained, "the restrictions that [the Marcellin-Fontanet circulars] entail for immigration, the administrative procedures that they impose, are going to complicate further the tasks, which are already very complex, of many of our enterprises . . . [these measures] risk causing important delays for the launching of numerous construction operations" (Henneresse 1979:419).

Labor's position on the Marcellin-Fontanet circulars was more complex. Trade unions had been calling for a reduction in immigrant entries for almost a quarter of a century. For many years labor leaders had seen the process of regularization that encouraged undocumented immigration as the *bête noire* of France's entry policies. The CGT proclaimed that clandestine immigration "aggravates further the exploitation of these workers, puts them at the mercy of employers' rapaciousness, and drives them toward those squalid *bidonvilles*" (CGT 1967:467). Trade unions felt that large-scale immigration in general harmed French workers by reducing wages and undermining the bargaining position of labor organizations. Working together, government and business elites had "systematically accelerated" immigration in an attempt "to exert increased pressure on all workers [and] to reinforce the exploitation of the entire working class" (CGT 1972:450).

Thus it was hardly surprising that trade union leaders initially welcomed the new immigration restrictions outlined in the Marcellin-Fontanet circulars. Unions had been calling for these types of restrictions on clandestine immigration for quite some time (CEDETIM 1975: 362). But labor's support for the restrictions was short-lived. Immigrants threatened with expulsion under the new policy began to protest against the circulars, often targeting unions themselves in an attempt to gain organized labor's support. When three Tunisian immigrants facing expulsion staged a hunger strike in the CFDT's Parisian headquarters, the union quickly backed the foreigners in their demands for regularization.

French organized labor had long held a potentially contradictory position of opposing immigration while supporting immigrants. This means that the unions did not want to see any additional foreign workers enter the French labor market, but once they did, the unions professed solidarity with their fellow laborers in the internationalist tradition. The difficulty was that immigration and immigrant issues could not always be separated. The French state had long given residency and work permits to illegal aliens already installed in France in an attempt to encourage more foreign workers to immigrate. Conversely, and here was the rub for unions, the logic of the Marcellin-Fontanet circulars was that by denying work and residency permits to illegal aliens, that state hoped to discourage future clandestine entries.

Thus in the early 1970s, union leaders were forced to choose between opposing immigration or supporting immigrants. As immigrant workers developed into an increasingly important segment of the French labor force, labor organizations were becoming even keener on gaining immigrant support. But organized labor's standing with foreign workers was growing tenuous by the early 1970s. Immigrant workers were no longer a quiescent group (Miller 1981). Starting with the protests of 1968, foreign workers fought vigorously for their own rights and interests. Immigrant labor strikes took on an anti-union tone. Foreign workers often mobilized outside the auspices of established trade unions in order to have their own grievances addressed. Small leftist groups supplied immigrant strikers with financial and organizational resources. Much to the dismay of union leaders, immigrants were able on several occasions to stop production in factories dominated by the major trade unions without their support. To bring immigrants back into the fold, trade unions became far more responsive to the specific needs of foreign workers and incorporated their demands (Miller 1981:91).

By the time the Marcellin-Fontanet circulars were issued, trade unions were bent on fostering stronger ties with immigrants. When forced to choose between the restrictions on clandestine immigration they had demanded and the support of immigrants they wanted, trade union leaders put solidarity with foreign workers first. In January 1973 the CGT and the CFDT issued a joint statement demanding that the government rescind the Marcellin-Fontanet circulars and regularize immigrants already residing in France (Minces 1973:143). Until these immigrants were regularized, the unions demanded that no additional foreign workers be allowed to come to France and that employers who continued to recruit foreign labor be sanctioned. The CGT and CFDT now condemned the circulars as nothing short of "hunting for immigrants," and threatened mass protests if the circulars were not repealed (CEDETIM 1975:362).

Would the unions' objections carry sufficient weight? For twenty-five years, the labor movement had opposed France's liberal immigration policies in vain. One labor leader, Marcel Dufriche, summed up the futility of the unions' efforts when he told the CGT's national congress, "Certainly the working class does not have an interest in massive immigration, but practically it cannot possibly stop it" (CGT 1963:131). But now labor's protests, combined with those of employers, would carry significant weight. The French government was unwilling to implement its will unilaterally in the face of strong opposition from both business and labor.

In light of the social partner's opposition to the new immigration measures, France's new minister of labor, Georges Gorse, met with employer and labor union representatives in May 1973. The following month, Gorse issued a circular that undid the Marcellin-Fontanet measures, at least temporarily, by granting an amnesty to immigrants residing illegally in France. The Gorse circular reopened the regularization process, and the number of immigrants who were granted legal status through regularization jumped from roughly 18,000 in the first half of 1973 to over 50,000 for the second half of the year (Henneresse 1979:422). Future illegal immigrants would have to confront the new limits on undocumented aliens, but those already residing in France were excluded by virtue of the Gorse circular.

Certainly, the trade unions' opposition to the Marcellin-Fontanet circulars must have come as something of a surprise to public officials. Labor leaders, after all, had been calling for the type of measures embodied in the circulars for twenty-five years, only to oppose them once they were issued. Prior consultation might have given the government more insight into labor's reasoning on this matter. It did not help matters that tripartite representation on the ONI's administrative council had been abolished since 1948. This situation was not lost on state elites during the policy crisis of the early 1970s. After meeting with business and labor leaders and rescinding the Marcellin-Fontanet circulars, Gorse proposed to the Council of Ministers that the government integrate employers and trade unions into the immigration policy-making process in a formal and permanent way in order to avoid future miscommunication (Benoît 1973). To this end the state created two new neo-corporatist institutions, a National Commission of Foreign Labor and a consultative committee designed to work with the ONI. The Ministry of Labor explicitly stated that these new bodies were "intended to involve the social partners in the elaboration and application of immigration policy" (Ministère du Travail 1976).

THE IMMIGRATION BAN

True to France's statist tradition, the government had formulated the Marcellin-Fontanet policies unilaterally and had moved decisively to implement these policies via administrative circulars. However, the combined

Table 6.1
Unemployment Rate in France, 1970–1979

Year	Unemployment Rate	% Change Since 1970
1970	1.7%	--
1971	2.3%	+35.3%
1972	2.4%	+41.2%
1973	2.1%	+23.5%
1974	2.3%	+35.3%
1975	3.7%	+117.6%
1976	4.4%	+158.8%
1977	4.8%	+182.4%
1978	4.8%	+182.4%
1979	5.6%	+229.4%

Source: OECD 1984

pressure of union and employer interests forced the state to abandon the Marcellin-Fontanet restrictions on illegal aliens and to offer a general amnesty. Still, state elites feared that continued large-scale immigration in the face of anticipated economic difficulties would be disastrous. In the end, the economic downturn that French state elites had anticipated did indeed take place. An unanticipated and dramatic increase in world oil prices exacerbated France's economic difficulties. Oil-producing nations acted in concert to hike the price of petroleum from $1.80 per barrel in February 1971 to $11.65 by December 1973 (Spero and Hart 1997:280–281). Unemployment rose from 1.7 percent in 1970 to 3.7 percent in 1975, and it would continue in an upward trajectory to 5.6 percent in 1979 (see Table 6.1). The confluence of the oil crisis and rising unemployment, along with stagnant economic growth and high rates of inflation, threw the French economy into a full-blown crisis.

Georges Pompidou's death in 1974 forced new elections, which were won by Pompidou's former minister of finance, Valéry Giscard d'Estaing. In office, Giscard and his executive cabinet moved swiftly to restrict immigration. Once again, the French government worked in the statist tradition of formulating policy unilaterally, without parliamentary discussion, and implemented new measures via administrative memoranda. In July 1974, the Council of Ministers announced that it had ratified the suspension of almost all immigration to France. The government's aim was to limit the entries of foreign workers and their families to correspond to employment opportunities. Only seasonal workers, citizens of the European Economic Community, and a few special categories (artists or workers with specialized skills) were exempted from the ban. The government's suspension of immigration was present as a temporary measure that would be reexamined after a few months. But it soon became clear that the suspension of immigration was more than a stop-gap measure. To coordinate the state's efforts, Giscard created the post of Secretary of State for Immigrant Workers (*Secrétaire d'Etat chargé des travailleurs immigrés*), and appointed André Postel-Vinay to the position. Postel-Vinay told the French daily *Le Monde* that it would be "indefensible" to allow immigrants to enter while unemployment was rising (*Le Monde*, September 24, 1974). In October 1974 the government announced that after taking economic conditions into consideration, it had decided to maintain the immigration ban for the foreseeable future.

French political elites were also aware of the interrelationship between immigration and other domestic problems. The housing crisis was clearly on the minds of government officials, and the Council of Ministers pledged to strongly augment its efforts to improve the immigrant housing situation at the same meeting where it announced the ban. The growing incidences of violent attacks against immigrants also influenced state elites. "You can imagine the social tensions that could be created" by allowing immigration to continue while unemployment rose, Postel-Vinay said in justification of the state's new restrictions (*Le Monde*, September 24, 1974).

Most employers wanted France to continue large-scale immigration. In the midst of the oil crisis, Yvon Chotard, a high-ranking CNPF official, asserted, "The French economy today needs foreign workers" (*Le Monde*, September 21, 1973). At its 1974 national meeting, the CNPF discussed the dangers of labor shortages (Freeman 1979:208). The CNPF warned that if the current sources of immigrant labor were exhausted, French economic production would stall. The CNPF also feared that sending states might form a cartel and set onerous conditions for allowing their nationals to emigrate to advanced industrialized nations. State elites had consulted with business leaders before implementing the ban and had characterized the measures as a temporary move. Nonetheless, numerous business interests mobilized in opposition to the ban, with some of the loudest objections coming from the Parisian Construction Federation (FPB), the Lourraine Federation of the BTP, the Federation of Cleaning Enterprises, the car manufacturer Peugeot, and the country's largest agricultural association, the *Fédération Nationale des Syndicats d'Exploitants Agricoles*, or FNSEA (Henneresse 1979:429). In a clever move that grabbed some attention, the FPB told employers to send photocopies of job listings to the government to demonstrate that they could not find the workers they needed.

Labor leaders, on the other hand, reacted somewhat cautiously. They had unexpectedly been forced to recant their initial support for the

Table 6.2
Immigration to France, 1970–1979

Year	Legal Immigration	% Change Since 1970
1970	255,195	--
1971	217,500	-14.8%
1972	173,029	-32.2%
1973	204,702	-19.8%
1974	132,499	-48.1%
1975	67,415	-73.6%
1976	84,286	-70.0%
1977	75,074	-70.6%
1978	58,479	-77.1%
1979	56,695	-77.8%

Source: OMI 1994

Marcellin-Fontanet restrictions, and they did not want to make a similar mistake this time around. Still, trade unions tentatively backed France's new immigration restrictions. In a measured response, the CGT stated that the suspension constituted only "the beginning of a real policy on the matter" (Benoît 1974:24). Some years later, Michèle Bonnechère would explain the CGT's position: "[The immigration ban] was understandable, since unemployment was increasing . . . that is why labor organizations did not contest this decision" (Weil 1988:181). *Force Ouvrière* had been demanding an immigration stoppage since September 1973, and it voiced support for restrictions, asserting that the state needed to limit "the migratory flux in the interest of all workers" (*Le Monde*, July 6, 1974:24). The ban ultimately solicited labor support because it allowed trade unions to back limits on immigration without alienating foreigners who were already part of the French work force.

The restrictions placed on immigration were comprehensive and effective. Looking back on the first ten months of the immigration stoppage, the Council of Ministers concluded that the decision to suspend immigration had been implemented rigorously. This rigorous implementation continued throughout the decade. The number of immigrant workers who came to settle permanently in France decreased from 174,243 in 1970 to 17,370 in 1980, for a staggering reduction of 90 percent over the course of the decade (see Table 6.2). The state also greatly curtailed the number of immigrants entering for the purpose of family reunification in spite of a ruling by

France's highest administrative court, the *Conseil d'Etat*, that families had a right to reunite. Over the course of the decade, family immigration was cut in half, dropping from 80,952 in 1970 to 42,020 in 1980 (OMI 1994). The only influx allowed to continue relatively unscathed during this period was that of seasonal workers, although these numbers fell slightly as well over the course of the 1970s, decreasing from about 135,000 in 1970 to roughly 120,000 in 1980 (OMI 1994).

France's shift from large-scale immigration to an outright ban highlighted both the statist institutional arrangements that characterized decision-making in this area and the neo-corporatist constraints on state action. The failure of the Marcellin-Fontanet circulars demonstrated that the state was hesitant to act unilaterally. Rather, it sought societal support from either capital or labor. From the end of the war until the early 1970s, it appeared to many that the coalition between the state and employers was a permanent, structural feature of French immigration policy, and that the trade unions held little sway. However, the immigration ban of 1974 illustrated that the state was willing to act against the interests and demands of business, provided that it was backed by labor. In this way France's neo-corporatist power relations gave the state considerable flexibility. Whether it wanted to restrict or to expand immigration, the state was able to garner the support of at least one social partner, which was all it needed.

IN THE WAKE OF THE BAN

France's decision to suspend immigration in 1974 marked a significant rupture in its postwar policies. The ban itself engendered a great many changes in the politics of immigration. One of the unexpected consequences of the immigration stoppage was that it helped to stabilize the nation's foreign population (Wihtol de Wenden, 1988:191). Whereas before a considerable number of immigrant workers returned periodically to their countries of origin, after the ban fewer immigrants opted to leave France, even for a short period of time, because they feared that they would not be allowed to reenter once they left. As the immigrant population stabilized, the ratio of women to men in the foreign community rose from 70:100 in 1975 to 76:100 in 1982 (Noiriel 1988:253). This settlement process was not only demographic, but psychological and political as well. Many foreigners abandoned the idea that they would one day return to their homelands. More and more, immigrant mobilization centered on issues concerning their political, social, and economic lives in France, and consequently their activity geared toward their homelands declined (Ireland 1994:50).

By presenting the immigration ban as a palliative for the country's economic woes, the government had implicitly placed at least some of the blame for France's difficulties on immigrants. But if immigrants did indeed harm the French economy, as the government's pronouncements and actions implied, there was little that could be done about it in terms of entry policies after 1974. The state had already suspended immigration in a comprehensive and effective manner. The number of immigrant workers coming to France was reduced by 90 percent over the course of the decade, and the number of immigrant workers' family members who came to join them was cut in half. Others who still came legally were mostly members of exempted groups such as artists or workers with specialized technical skills, or citizens of EEC member countries who were guaranteed the right to immigrate to France by instrument of international treaties. Overall, few were exempted from the suspension, and thus the state would have been hard-pressed to reduce legal immigration any further.

Having already cut off much of the immigration flow, and with the economic situation worsening in spite of the suspension, state elites called for a reduction in the immigrant population already living in France. Foreigners, many public officials were now saying, should return from whence they came. In April 1975, Paul Dijoud proclaimed in an immigrant shantytown that "all the unemployed in this town would be inclined to return to their countries if their travel expenses were paid" (Weil 1991:96). In January 1976, Prime Minister Jacques Chirac, foreshadowing the rhetoric of the National Front, told a national television audience, "A country in which there are 900,000 unemployed, but where there are more than two million immigrants, is not a country in which the unemployment problem is unsolvable" (Wihtol de Wenden 1988:206). The following month, Labor Minister Michel Durafour echoed Chirac's sentiments when he wrote, "Why hide it, the employment situation in France is absurd: there are one million unemployed. But at the same time there are two million foreign workers" (Wihtol de Wenden 1988:206).

The state had run into insurmountable opposition in 1972 when it tried to enact policies that could lead to the expulsion of immigrants already residing in France. However, unlike the Marcellin-Fontanet policies, the state first tried to induce voluntary repatriations in the wake of the ban. In 1977, France's new Prime Minister, Raymond Barre, along with the new Secretary of State for Foreign Workers, Lionel Stoléru, introduced the *"aide au retour"* program that would offer 10,000 francs to foreigners in exchange for their permanent departure. The program did enjoy some success as roughly 100,000 people accepted the money (Ireland 1994:49). But the program largely missed its target audience. Although the *aide au retour* program was designed to encourage unemployed immigrants of African origin to repatriate, most who took the state up on its offer were employed and from the Iberian peninsula (Ireland 1994:49). In 1980, the state deemed Iberians ineligible for the program, and the following year the program was terminated.

With so few immigrants willing to return to their countries of origin voluntarily, and with unemployment continuing to climb, the French state decided to organize the forced departures of hundreds of thousands of legal aliens in 1978. State elites devised a two-pronged strategy: they would refrain from renewing residency permits, and they would expand the powers of the Minister of the Interior to deport immigrants (Weil 1991:115). The plan was to rid France of 200,000 immigrants per year (Money 1999:112). But such policies would obviously affect the countries to which migrants would be sent, and this factor placed constraints on what the French state could do. Citizens of EEC countries were exempted from this planned mass expulsion, as were Spanish and Portuguese nationals whose homelands were scheduled to join the EEC. The Evian Agreements of 1962, which ended the war between France and Algeria, prevented France from deporting Algerians against their will. Nonetheless, there were many immigrants who did not enjoy the protection of international treaties, and even those who were protected feared the worst.

As had been the case when the Marcellin-Fontanet circulars were issued, trade unions mobilized to protect foreign workers who were already part of the French labor market. The CGT, CFDT and FO all fought against the proposed deportation plans. French labor leaders coordinated their efforts with unions of nationals from Algeria, Spain, Italy, Morocco, and Portugal to sponsor a mass, international protest against the planned deportations (Weil 1991:129). Faced with such strong opposition, the state capitulated and cancelled its plans for compulsory returns.

Perhaps the most important development in the politics of immigration after the 1974 suspension, at least from an institutional perspective, was the rise of the State Council (*Conseil d'État*), France's highest administrative court, as a powerful and separate state actor. In the late 1970s, the Council annulled attempts by the state to stop family reunification, including measures that were part of the July 1974 circulars (Hollifield 1992: 187). The Council also ruled against the *aide au retour* program. All together, the Council nullified over a dozen circulars issued by the government from 1975 until the mid-1980s (Ireland 1994:49). In general, the Council ruled not against the policies per se, but against the way in which these policies were made. Policy, the court ruled, could not be instituted by instrument of unpublished circulars. Instead, policy-making was a right and an obligation of the French parliament, and thus the government needed to pass its immigration policy proposals through the National Assembly and the Senate (Money 1999:112). The Giscard-Barre government was able to reinstate most of the policies annulled by the court, but had to do so by proposing bills (*projets de loi*) that the National Assembly passed into law. For the first time in the postwar era, the French state was fractured in a significant way concerning immigration policy. The Council's decisions inhibited the government from enacting immigration laws in a technocratic manner. From this point on, entry and incorporation policies would have to pass through the legislature, and this was sure to politicize immigration issues to a far greater extent than they had been.

CONCLUSION

The French government's move to restrict the entry of foreign workers and their families in the 1970s was a telling episode. Before France (as well as other countries such as West Germany and Switzerland) decided to suspend immigration, many analysts had come to view large-scale labor immigration as a constituent component of advanced industrialized economies. In their landmark study, *Immigrant Workers and Class Structure in Western Europe*, Stephen Castles and Godula Kosack asserted that "immigrant workers have become a structural necessity for the economies of receiving countries" (Castles and Kosack 1973:25). In light of the increasing dependence of advanced industrialized nations on foreign labor during the 1950s and 1960s, it is easy to understand why analysts would draw such conclusions. But France's suspension of immigration in 1974, a move that reduced permanent labor immigration by roughly 90 percent, contradicted the widespread consensus that wealthy capitalist nations needed to import large quantities of cheap, exploitable foreign labor on an annual basis. Over the last quarter century, capitalism in France and other western European nations has survived without recourse to large-scale immigration.

France's suspension of immigration also demonstrated that the French state was an autonomous actor—one that had its own interests and was capable of pursuing its own goals. The state proved not to be controlled by employers, and when the government's policy preferences diverged from those of business, public officials acted accordingly. At the time of the immigration stoppage, employers were predicting that there would be a shortage of foreign labor over the coming decade, and they argued that additional steps were necessary to recruit foreign labor. But state elites believed France needed to implement restrictive measures. Employers mobilized to protest the ban, but the "effects of employers' lobbying appears to have been limited, at least so far as a formal change in policy is concerned" (Hollifield 1992:81).

Why did France stop the influx of foreign workers in 1974? Clearly, this seems to be an example of economic conditions determining immigration policy outcomes. But the question is why? As we have seen in this chapter, France's institutional arrangement played a critical role in translating economic difficulties into restrictive immigration laws. Statist institutional structures furnished France with a relatively unitary and autonomous governmental apparatus that took measures to restrict immigration in the face of an economic downturn. These policies were enacted by simple administrative decree, with the Council of Ministers issuing circulars that were never even published. This was the case with Marcellin-Fontanet circulars, the Gorse circular, and the series of circulars issued in July 1974 that collectively constituted the so-called French immigration ban. There was no separation of powers, and thus no power basis within the state from which opponents of restrictions might resist the new restrictions. There was no parliamentary debate, let alone parliamentary action. Another concomitant and important factor was that French political institutions insulated officials from societal and political pressures, thus encouraging political elites to make decisions in a technocratic manner, based predominantly on economic considerations.

But we have also seen that that the state did not operate in a vacuum. French institutional arrangements gave some measure of power and influence to labor and business interests. Hence the state faced certain neo-corporatist constraints, and immigration policy-making exhibited some neo-corporatist dynamics. The Marcellin-Fontanet ordeal spoke to the limits placed on state action by employers and trade unions. Faced with strong opposition from both business and labor interests, the state rescinded the Marcellin-Fontanet restrictions, at least temporarily, by instituting an amnesty by instrument of the Gorse circular. The state, nonetheless, was in a strategically advantageous position. If formulated carefully, immigration restrictions were highly likely to garner trade union support. When the state suspended immigration in 1974, it did so with the support of the major trade unions, and over the objections of many employers.

Chapter 7

The New Politics of French Immigration

In the 1980s and 1990s unemployment in France soared to over ten percent of the active population, and the dearth of jobs appeared to become a structural feature of the French economy. In light of this development, state elites, union representatives, and even business leaders supported the nation's closed borders policy, and the 1974 "ban" prohibiting most immigrant entries remained in place during the final two decades of the twentieth century. With questions of immigrant entries seemingly settled for the foreseeable future, debates over immigration turned increasingly toward issues that concerned immigrants and immigrant communities that were already established in France. Moreover, French immigration was transformed from a largely technical issue managed in an administrative manner into a highly charged political issue that provoked bitter divisions within the nation.

As immigration became one of the most salient public questions in France, the political dynamics surrounding the issue were profoundly altered. From the end of World War II until the 1980s, a strong, unitary state, somewhat constrained by labor and business interests, dominated French immigration politics. But institutional changes over the final two decades of the century began to erode what we have referred to as the statist-corporatist dynamics of French immigration policy-making. A series of rulings by the French courts beginning in the 1970s annulled immigration laws implemented by administrative memoranda, and this began a process that fractured the French state on these issues. The very fact that the judiciary asserted such unprecedented independence was itself an act of divided decision-making and of divided government. Furthermore, the substance of the courts' rulings—in essence declaring that the executive and administrative method of immigration policy-making was unconstitutional and that parliamentary action on these issues was required—pushed immigration policy-making into the more divisive and more partisan sphere of legislative deliberation and decision-making. This institutional change contributed to the politicization of immigration policy, and it was one of the reasons that immigration increasingly became an object of party competition.

Another important institutional change occurred when François Mitterrand and his Socialist government repealed laws that prevented foreigners from forming civic associations. With these institutional constraints removed, immigrant organizations proliferated, and a new set of political actors started to join business and labor interests in the immigration policy-making arena. Then, in 1985, President Mitterrand altered France's electoral institutions in a way that made it easier for small parties to gain representation. This benefited the extreme-right National Front, and provided it with a national audience for its anti-immigrant proposals. The rise of the National Front and its leader, Jean-Marie Le Pen, further politicized immigration issues. As a result of all these developments, governmental elites could no longer regulate immigration in a technocratic manner. Instead, in the 1980s and 1990s immigration became, in the words of Monique Chemillier-Gendreau (1998), "a privileged object of ideological manipulation." Suddenly, immigration policy became as symbolic as it was instrumental.

Thus by the 1990s the politics of immigration seemed thoroughly transformed. A far wider array of actors—including immigrant associations, political parties, and different branches of government—were now struggling over how to deal with France's immigrant population (many of whom were actually not immigrants at all, but the children of immigrants). But even with the new actors and new approaches to the issues, the extent of the transformation is not yet clear. It remains to be seen whether these new players will have a say in the making of immigrant entry policies, or whether the old triad of government, business, and labor will retain its control over the nation's borders.

THE ASCENT OF THE SOCIALISTS

In 1981 François Mitterrand, the Socialist Party (*Parti Socialiste*, or PS) candidate, defeated Valéry Giscard d'Estaing in the presidential campaign. Upon taking office, President Mitterrand dissolved the National Assembly, as was his constitutional right, and called for new elections. Candidates from the PS and the French Communist Party (*Parti Communiste Français*, or PCF) won a combined majority in parliament. The two parties overcame their differences to form a governing coalition of the left, and Pierre Mauroy of the PS was named prime minister. During his campaign, Mitterrand had condemned societal racism and criticized the Giscard government's treatment of immigrant workers. Although immigration issues were not Mitterrand's highest priority, he nonetheless promised that a Socialist government would suppress discrimination, guarantee equal rights to immigrant workers, and grant foreign residents the right to vote in municipal elections—all in an attempt to integrate France's foreign population.

The Mauroy government had no intention of lifting the immigration ban. In June 1981 François Autain, the new Secretary of State for Immigration, told the public that the leftist government would fight to keep new immigrants out while working to integrate those already residing in France (Ireland, 1994:61). In terms of entry policies, public officials planned few changes. But the Socialist-Communist government did plan on altering how the state dealt with its existing immigrant population. The year he took office, Mitterrand signaled his commitment to racial and ethnic harmony by creating the post of Minister of National Solidarity. The first official to hold this office, Nicole Questiaux, proclaimed that "it is solidarity with all, French and immigrant, without discrimination . . . that will guide our actions" (Weil 1991:139). The government moved quickly to end the so-called *aide au retour* program that paid immigrants to return to their countries of origin. The Mauroy government also ceased the forced expulsions that the Giscard government had carried out on a limited basis.

Meanwhile, the immigrant population in France, while sizeable, was stabilizing. All things considered, the 1974 immigration stoppage had been quite effective at limiting the number of foreign laborers legally entering the country, reducing the number of immigrant workers who came each year to settle permanently in France from a high of 174,243 in 1970 to 17,370 in 1980 (OMI 1994). The reduction in those who came annually to reunite with their families was significant as well, falling from a high of 81,496 in 1971 to 42,020 in 1980 (OMI 1994). But the nation still faced pressing issues surrounding its foreign population, especially the large and growing population of illegal aliens. Many immigrants had avoided entry restrictions in the 1970s by coming to France without papers, and the accumulation of these illegal immigrants produced a significant clandestine population by the time Mitterrand took office.

Trade unions fought to protect these undocumented residents. In 1981 labor representatives met with government officials to urge them to institute an amnesty that would regularize the status of illegal immigrants. In order to facilitate the process, labor leaders lobbied the government to accept the testimony of co-workers or neighbors as proof that an immigrant was employed in cases where employers refused to provide a work contract (Haus 1999:709). Unions also worked to ease the long and difficult application process by persuading the state to increase the number of civil servants dealing with the issue (Haus 1999:709).

Mitterrand himself supported an amnesty for undocumented foreign workers and their families. However, several members of the Council of Ministers were hesitant to grant such an amnesty because they feared that it would encourage further illegal immigration, and that the resulting increased influx would exacerbate France's unemployment problem (Weil 1991:148). But in France's dual executive system, the president usually dictates policy-making when his party controls the National Assembly. In the end, the government went along with Mitterrand's proposal and instituted a one-time regularization program open to all immigrants who had arrived in France before January 1, 1981. To prevent further illegal entries, the government warned that such a program would not be offered again. Trade unions worked with the state to assure the program's success. Unions helped undocumented workers fill out the necessary forms and submitted the forms on their behalf, thus acting as an authorized intermediary body between immigrants and the state (Haus 1999:709). This amnesty regularized roughly 130,000 illegal immigrants by 1983 (Dionne 1983:A2).

Another aspect of Mitterrand's strategy to integrate the immigrant population into French society was to enfranchise foreigners at the local level. Public opinion opposed such a move. Polls showed 58 percent of the public against granting voting rights to non-citizens, while only 35 percent supported such measures (Weil 1991:160). The Mitterrand government was well aware of this, but unorganized preferences had little direct impact on immigration policy decisions. In August 1981, Foreign Minister Claude Cheysson announced that the government intended to proceed with its plan to grant the right to vote in local elections to legal immigrants who had resided in France for at least five years.

However, there was a strong political backlash from organized interests, especially political parties, against this proposal to enfranchise foreigners. The recently defeated parties of the center-right, the Union for French Democracy (*Union pour la Démocratie Française*, or UDF) and the Gaullist party, the Rally for the Republic (*Rassemblement pour la République*, or RPR), lashed out against the plan. Jacques Chirac, mayor of Paris and leader of the RPR, maintained that the right to vote was intricately tied to citizenship and could not be given to non-citizens (Weil 1991:158–159). There was also considerable opposition to the proposal within the governing coalition. The Socialist Party's coalition partners, the PCF, argued that there was no demand for such a policy (Weil 1991:158). Mitterrand and Mauroy were already embattled over much more visible proposals such as the nationalization of private industries and enormous tax increases. They had to choose their political fights. With strong opposition to the enfranchisement proposal from both their foes and their allies, and with so little to gain by enacting it, Mitterrand and his cabinet let the issue drop. Clearly, what was once a policy area dealt with in an "executive and administrative style" was slowly becoming an object of party competition.

Mitterrand was able to expand immigrants' rights in an area that was far less controversial than voting, but which was still important. On October 9, 1981, the government enacted an Association Law that for the first time allowed foreigners to form associations in France under the same rules that governed citizens. These new immigrant associations were thereafter eligible to receive public funding. Portuguese, Spanish, Turkish, Algerian, Moroccan, and Asian immigrants, among others, formed new organizations, often along national lines, and within a few years there were over 4,200 of these heretofore forbidden organizations (Ireland 1994:63–64). The Association Law was important not just for the new rights it extended to immigrants, but also for its more far-reaching potential to change the dynamics of the policy-making process. French political institutions had made it very difficult for groups other than business and labor interests to influence immigration policies, especially entry policies. The new law repealed the Daladier decree of 1939 that had forbidden foreign associations on French soil. With important institutional obstacles removed, newly formed ethnic associations had the potential to alter the landscape of actors vying to influence immigration policy.

In June 1982 the Mitterrand government took one more step toward expanding immigrants' rights, this time in the area of industrial relations. The so-called Auroux Laws strengthened the rights of foreign workers *qua* workers. The new policies removed the French language requirements of immigrants to run for seats in employee institutions. In addition, foreign workers became eligible for the first time to sit on important industrial relations councils known as the *Conseils des Prud'hommes*.

All things considered, although immigrant issues were not a top priority, the Socialist-Communist government took several important steps to improve the lives of immigrants working and residing in France during the first two years of leftist rule. But by 1983 the tide began to turn. Mitterrand's economic program, which centered on nationalizing industry and increasing both taxes and state expenditures, was failing miserably, even by his own eventual admission. Unemployment continued to climb, rising from 6.3 percent in 1980 to 8.3 percent in 1983 (see Table 7.1). The center-right opposition condemned the Socialists for not doing enough to keep immigrants out or to expel undocumented foreigners (Dionne 1983:A2). In municipal elections in 1983, many local politicians verbally attacked the immigrant population. Le Pen and his followers in the National Front portrayed foreigners as a criminal element contaminating France, and blamed foreign workers for much of France's economic woes.

Responding to these developments, the Socialist government adopted a tougher stand against immigrants. Georgina Dufoix, the Secretary of State for Families, Population, and Foreign Workers, told a magazine journalist

Table 7.1
Unemployment Rate in France, 1980–1989

Year	Unemployment Rate	% Change Since 1980
1980	6.3%	--
1981	7.4%	+17.5%
1982	8.1%	+28.6%
1983	8.3%	+31.7%
1984	9.7%	+54.0%
1985	10.2%	+61.9%
1986	10.4%	+65.1%
1987	10.5%	+66.7%
1988	10.0%	+58.7%
1989	9.4%	+49.2%

Source: OECD 1999

that immigrants "should respect French laws and French habits of life" (Dionne 1983:A2). In August 1983 the Council of Ministers voted to tighten border patrols, to sanction employers who hired undocumented immigrants, and to expel illegal aliens. The government also moved to limit family immigration, to end regularizations, and to establish committees at the departmental level to combat illegal immigration. On November 4, 1983, Dufoix asserted, "The regularization that we conducted [in 1981–1982] was certainly exceptional: there will not be another" (Wihtol de Wenden, 1988:295). Dufoix also raised the idea of bringing back the *"aide au retour"* program, but opposition from countries to which immigrants would be returning put a damper on this proposal (Weil 1991:174–175).

With the immigration ban still in place, there was little room for further restrictions. The Mitterrand government cut immigration where it could, but the slight reductions could not have had much impact on the French economy. The number of immigrants who came to settle permanently was reduced from 18,483 in 1983 to 10,959 in 1985, but this was probably as low as it could possibly go (OMI 1994). Immigrants from European Community (EC) nations could not be kept out according to EC law. Another important category of immigrants consisted of those who came for the purpose of reuniting with their family in France. The Constitutional Council had ruled that the state could not end family reunions. Still, the French state searched for ways to reduce this influx. On December 4, 1984, the government issued a decree that required applicants for family reunion to

Table 7.2
Family Migration to France, 1980–1989

Year	Family Immigration	% Change Since 1980
1980	42,020	--
1981	41,589	-1.0%
1982	47,396	+12.8%
1983	45,767	+8.9%
1984	39,621	-5.7%
1985	32,545	-22.5%
1986	27,140	-35.4%
1987	26,769	-36.3%
1988	29,345	-30.1%
1989	34,594	-17.7%

Source: OMI 1994

remain in their countries of origin while their applications were processed (Husbands 1991:184). This did manage to lessen family immigration from 45,767 in 1983 to 27,140 in 1986, but once again, given the court's decision, this was just about as low as it could go (see Table 7.2).

The employment situation in the mid-1980s deteriorated to the point where even French employers, who had traditionally fought for large-scale immigration, supported the state's attempts to block entries. In fact, some employers participated in efforts to reduce the French workforce. In May 1984, Citroën, Peugeot, and Talbot all signed up for a new type of industry-specific *aide au retour* program that sent immigrant workers back to their countries of origin (Weil 1991:183). Trade unions did not oppose the program on the grounds that it was voluntary and that no untoward pressure was being placed on foreign workers to participate (Weil 1991: 183).

THE EMERGENCE OF THE NATIONAL FRONT

One of the most important developments in immigration politics during the 1980s was the rise of the far-right National Front. The *Front National* (FN) continued a long tradition of extreme nationalism in France. In the second half of the twentieth century this tradition can be traced from the Nazi collaborators of the Vichy regime, to the Poujardist movement of the 1950s, to the colonialists who planned to overthrow the government rather than surrender France's overseas empire, to the various neo-fascist organizations that united as the FN in 1972. At first, the FN was singularly unsuccessful in the electoral arena. Jean-Marie Le Pen, the FN's charismatic leader, received 0.75 percent of the vote in France's 1974 presidential election (Singer, 1991:372). In 1981 Le Pen failed to collect the 500 signatures from elected officials to appear on the presidential ballot.

After beating the anti-communist drum in vain for nearly a decade, in the early 1980s Le Pen and the FN changed tactics and began to focus their attacks on immigrants (Taguieff 1985). To be sure, they were not the only ones. Parties of the mainstream right, particularly the RPR and the UDR, reproached the Socialist government for being lax on clandestine entries, notwithstanding the fact that the mainstream right had presided over decades of illegal immigration that they not only condoned but encouraged. And on the far left, the French Communist Party railed against immigrants and the harm they allegedly did to French workers, particularly during the 1981 presidential campaign, before they joined the government (Schain 1987:239). But it was the far-right FN that was able to capitalize most on this issue by ratcheting up the rhetoric to a xenophobic level where most members of the mainstream right and far left refused to tread. To Le Pen, immigrants were dirty foreign invaders "who want to sleep in my bed, with my wife" (Singer, 1991:373). Le Pen proposed ending all state benefits for legal immigrants and sending them back to their countries of origin. Le Pen also embraced anti-Semitic positions such as denying the Nazi genocide against Jews.

In 1983 the FN finally found some political traction in municipal elections. Law-and-order issues played a major role in local elections that year, and FN candidates pointed to foreigners as the cause of rising crime rates. Of particular importance was the September election in Dreux, a town near Paris. In the first ballot, the lists of the mainstream left and right won handily, receiving 42.7 percent and 40.6 percent of the vote, respectively (Singer, 1991:373). In the second ballot, the mainstream right merged its list with that of the National Front, which had won 16.7 percent in the first round (Singer, 1991:373). The combined right-wing slate won the runoff and, more importantly, the FN had gained a certain degree of legitimacy.

The FN was able to build quickly on this newfound success and legitimacy. In the June 1984 election for seats in the European Parliament, Le Pen's party won over 11 percent of the vote in France. Ironically, the surge in the FN's popularity was partially the product of the left's rise to power. Some FN voters were conservatives who wanted to oppose the left more vigorously than the mainstream right was doing at the time (Singer, 1991: 374). The FN also appealed to voters who had lost or feared losing their jobs, voters who wanted France to get tougher on crime, voters who lamented the decline of traditional values of "God, country, and family," and, of course, those who resented or even hated immigrants and their children (Safran 1998:96–97).

By the mid-1980s the National Front was building a modest base of support, but its emergence in the national and international limelight came about abruptly—largely as an unintended consequence of institutional change. After half a decade in power, the Socialists' popularity was in rapid decline. The party's failed economic program and the persistence of high unemployment rates seemed likely to doom the PS in the 1986 National Assembly elections. In 1985 François Mitterrand, widely acknowledged as an extraordinary political tactician, pushed for a law that would eliminate France's single-member district system for choosing members of the National Assembly and replace it with a proportional representation system in time for the country's imminent parliamentary elections. The new electoral system did not prevent the mainstream right from gaining a majority, but it did mute their victory by producing a smaller governing majority than they would have had under the old single-district, winner-take-all system. The new system allowed smaller parties, like the FN, to gain seats in the National Assembly at the expense of larger parties. When the smoke cleared, thirty-five members of the National Front, led by Jean-Marie Le Pen—an open admirer of Generals Pinochet and Franco, and a man who once called the Holocaust a mere detail of World War II—were members of France's National Assembly. The FN was finally a national party, with newfound legitimacy to go along with a sizeable delegation to France's most powerful legislative body.

COHABITATION

In 1986 the mainstream right coalition of the RPR and UDF won a majority in the National Assembly. The Socialist leader, François Mitterrand, still had two years left in his term, and thus the Fifth Republic's first period of divided government, what the French called "cohabitation," was inaugurated. Under France's dual executive, the president managed to retain much of his role in international affairs, but the newly appointed prime minister, Jacques Chirac, and his cabinet assumed control of most domestic policy decisions, including immigration policy. What for thirty years had been a powerful presidency was transformed into a largely ceremonial position.

Prime Minister Chirac and his government moved quickly to fulfill promises it had made to take a tougher stand on immigration. Chirac and other leaders of the mainstream right had argued that immigration was exacerbating French unemployment and that lax immigration control rendered France vulnerable to terrorism. Although the number of immigrant entries was extremely low by historical and comparative standards, the Chirac government wanted to be seen as combating immigration.

In June 1986 the Council of Ministers adopted a new refugee policy that allowed border control officers to sort out and reject asylum seekers before they could be examined by the agency in charge of refugees, the *Office Français de Protection des Réfugiés et Apatrides* (OFPRA). In September of that year France reintroduced visa requirements. Consulates in North Africa thus became a first line of defense against entries from the Maghreb, where would-be immigrants now had to prove that they could be housed and supported financially before they were allowed to enter France (Schain 1990:257). Anti-immigration measures named after the hard-line Minister of the Interior, Charles Pasqua, were also passed in September 1986. The Pasqua Law strengthened border policing and made it much easier for the government to deport foreigners who had come illegally or who had been convicted of crimes. Largely as a consequence of the Pasqua Law, the number of immigrants refused entry in 1987 rose to over 71,000—an increase of 50 percent from the previous year (Schain 1990:258).

According to Chirac and his government, immigrants did not only threaten to take away jobs from French workers, they also threatened to dilute French national identity. France had a long tradition of absorbing foreigners. For two centuries French law had readily granted citizenship to immigrants who came to make their lives in France. French law had also automatically attributed French citizenship to anyone born on French soil—a principle known as *jus soli*. Having promised to take on the immigration issue during the election, the RPR-UDF government decided it was time to reexamine the acquisition of French citizenship by immigrants. Michel Hannoun of the RPR stated in October 1986 that the "passive acquisition of French nationality must be revised" (Husbands 1991:187). The Chirac government proposed abandoning *jus soli* and making it much more difficult for children born in France of immigrant parents to acquire French citizenship. President Mitterrand and the PS strongly opposed these measures, as did some members of the RPR and the UDF (Schain 1990:259). Chirac decided not to push the proposed legislation too strongly, and in 1987 his government appointed a Commission on Nationality (*Commission de la Nationalité*) to consider French naturalization laws. The commission's report supported much of what Chirac had proposed, but his government fell from power before it was able to enact any measures that would withhold French citizenship from the children of immigrants born in France.

MITTERRAND REDUX

François Mitterrand, taken for dead politically just a few years earlier, defeated Jacques Chirac in the 1988 presidential election. Mitterrand immediately dissolved the National Assembly, and the Socialist Party once again won a parliamentary majority. The new government, under the leadership of Prime Minister Michel Rocard of the PS, found itself in a very difficult position vis-à-vis the immigration issue—an issue that had become increasingly important in the public eye. Many in the PS leadership felt that immigrants, exploited for so long economically, were now being exploited politically as parties of the right competed to see who could gain the most by blaming immigrants and their children for France's economic and social woes. This was still a political party, after all, that proclaimed upon taking the reins of power in 1981 that "it is solidarity with all, French and immigrant, without discrimination . . . that will guide our actions." But by 1988, the PS was getting clobbered politically on the immigration issue. Many in the party, including Pierre Joxe, the Minister of the Interior, feared appearing "soft" on the immigration issue (Husbands 1991:189).

Rocard decided on a strategy that would repeal some of the more draconian aspects of the Pasqua Law while tightening controls against illegal entries, thus demonstrating that the PS could also be tough on clandestine immigration. Formulating immigration policy would be all the more difficult because it could no longer be implemented via administrative decree. Nonetheless, the Socialists were committed to amending the Pasqua Law. The proposed changes to the Pasqua Law were debated in the National Assembly in May 1989, and the revisions were just barely passed in early June by a vote of 278 to 270, with members of the Communist Party abstaining (Husbands 1991:190).

By 1990 racial tensions seemed to be spiraling out of control. In Marseilles (a city that had given Le Pen 28 percent of the vote in the 1988 presidential election), a police officer shot Saad Saoudi, an Algerian man, while he was in custody and handcuffed. In St. Florentin, a café owner shot two Arab youths in a dispute. In Roanne, a French driver deliberately ran down Majib Labdaoui, a Moroccan student living in France. Bombs destroyed several mosques across France. President Mitterrand lashed out against what he called "crimes of stupidity, brutality, and intolerance" (Ibrahim 1990:A2). Even Charles Pasqua condemned "this sort of racist fever," though many thought he had done much to inflame it (Ibrahim 1990: A2).

The Socialist government, searching for a way to combat xenophobia, offered a bill that would bar from elected office and from government jobs anyone who incited racial hatred—a measure directed at Le Pen and the FN. The National Assembly passed the bill by a vote of 307 to 265 on May 2, 1990, after a contentious debate. A few days later, in an incident that reverberated throughout France, over fifty graves were desecrated in two Jewish cemeteries. On May 14, François Mitterrand joined tens of thousands of people, along with representatives of every major political party with the exception of the National Front, in a silent march to protest the desecrations and racism in general.

Clearly, France had become home to a politically and socially significant xenophobic faction. In a 1990 poll, 16 percent of respondents supported mass deportations to rid France of its immigrant population (Riding 1990: 16). While most of the French population did not support such extreme measures, public resentment of France's immigrant population was widespread, and politicians of all stripes played to these feelings. In 1991 Jacques Chirac offered comments that could have been made by Le Pen, conjuring up images of an immigrant man with "three or four wives, some 20 children, that receives 50,000 francs per month in social welfare . . . Add to that the noise and the smell, and the French worker goes crazy" (Riding 1991a:9). Chirac placed the blame for what he called France's "overdose" of immigrants squarely on Mitterrand and the PS (Riding 1991a:9).

Edith Cresson of the PS replaced Rocard as France's prime minister in 1991. Cresson knew that she faced a very delicate situation as tensions rose in suburban housing projects where many immigrants and their offspring resided, and as violent clashes between police and young people of Arab descent proliferated. The overall French unemployment rate was 9.4 percent, and climbing (OECD 1999). Prime Minister Cresson and her government announced in June that they would augment police patrolling in 400 immigrant communities, while sending roughly 300,000 teenagers, on a voluntary basis, to summer camps in rural areas (Riding 1991a:9). In July Cresson let it be known that the government would enact stricter measures to prevent illegal immigration and charter planes to deport illegal immigrants (Riding 1991b:A5). The new measures included the possible expulsion of legal immigrants who hired illegal immigrants at illegally low wages, the issuing of transit visas with fixed dates of departure (rather than more open tourist visas) to foreigners who came from countries that were the source of many illegal immigrants, and the establishment of computerized immigration files that could be transmitted more quickly (Riding 1991b:A5). In a demonstration of the government's commitment to tighter controls, the number of foreigners detained for possible expulsion climbed from 9,641 in 1990 to 32,673 in 1991, although the number actually expelled only rose slightly from 4,567 to 5,867 (Schain 1993:76).

Harlem Désir, the head of S.O.S. Racism, condemned the measures. "We must not make immigrants the scapegoats of our social problems," Désir stated (Riding 1991b:A5). A mass anti-racist demonstration was held on January 25, 1992, to condemn the xenophobic rhetoric of the right and the repressive measures enacted by the governing left. The major trade unions, along with civil rights groups and some far-left political parties, organized the protest, which was attended by tens of thousands of people in Paris.

LA HAINE

In the 1993 parliamentary elections, the RPR-UDF coalition, known as the *Union pour la France du progrès* (UPF), put forth a common front and a common platform. The mainstream right promised legislation that would make it more difficult for children of immigrants to obtain French citizenship, new laws that would allow local officials to block family reunification, and new policies that would increase the apprehension and expulsion of undocumented foreigners (Schain 1993:73–74). In the contest, the UPF won a resounding victory, taking an incredible 85 percent of the seats in the National Assembly, and ousting the Socialists from power in convincing fashion. The UPF selected Edouard Balladur as the prime minister, and he wasted no time in announcing a major campaign to cut down on illegal immigration and on crime in immigrant neighborhoods. The shooting of an immigrant and the son of an immigrant almost immediately after the RPR-UDF coalition assumed office caused many to fear that the new government's arrival was taken by police as a green light to use greater force against minorities (Riding 1993a:A2). Fodé Sylla, the head of S.O.S. Racism, charged that "by confusing police precincts with sheriff's offices, the forces of order have been turned into cowboys" (Riding 1993a:A2).

The Balladur government moved immediately on the question of the attribution of French citizenship to the children of immigrants born in France. The Chirac government of 1986–1988 had handled this issue very cautiously, setting up a commission to study the issue and to engender public debate. With anti-immigrant sentiments ratcheting upward, the Balladur government showed no such hesitation. While not denying citizenship outright to second-generation immigrants, the UPF did pass a law that required the French-born children of immigrants to apply for French citizenship between the ages of sixteen and twenty-one, and in some cases they could be refused. This was the RPR-UDF's first piece of legislation, sending a clear signal that it was going to respond to the perceived immigration problem. The bill passed in a landslide vote, 473 to 92, and polls showed that roughly 75 percent of the French public supported the government's move (Riding 1993b:A8).

Another policy initiative of the new government was to instruct police to check the identification papers of anyone who "acted" foreign. The notion of acting foreign was used to protect the state from accusations of racial profiling, which French law prohibited. Charles Pasqua, appointed once again to the post of Minister of the Interior, was a strong supporter of this approach, which he claimed would help France achieve what he called "zero immigration." The government also moved against the limited number of legal immigrants who were allowed to enter the country. Balladur's cabinet instituted a new policy that required foreigners to remain at least two years in France before they were permitted to bring in relatives under the country's family reunification programs.

The Constitutional Council struck down some of the UPF's measures to limit immigration. The council annulled legislation in the spring of 1993 that would have allowed the state to jail some illegal immigrants for months without trial. Also annulled was a law that would have allowed authorities to refuse to issue marriage licenses if they suspected that the purpose of the union was for a foreigner to gain French citizenship. In the fall, the government passed the same measures in slightly modified form to comply with the council's ruling. The government threatened to alter the constitution to place greater limits on the council if it continued to block this legislation.

In September 1994 the government banned the wearing of Muslim head-scarves in France's public schools. Five years earlier, a principal had started a national debate by expelling three girls for wearing such scarves, claiming violation of the principle of secular education (Beriss 1990). The Council of State offered an ambiguous decision that said wearing religious symbols in school is perfectly legal, provided it does not interfere with other students' religious freedoms or education. For practical purposes, local school officials were subsequently given discretion over such issues. But the UPF claimed in 1994 that a uniform policy for all of France was in order. Education Minister François Bayrou declared that the purpose of the ban was to "build a united, secular society," and that France could not "accept ostentatious signs that divide our youth" (Ibrahim 1994:4).

In 1995, Jacques Chirac won the presidency, and he named Alain Juppé the prime minister. For the first time since 1981, France's mainstream right had control of both the presidency and parliament. The Juppé government set out quickly to show that it would be tough on immigration. Jean-Luis Debré, the newly appointed Interior Minister, announced in July that the state had already deported three planeloads of undocumented Africans.

In 1996 about 300 illegal immigrants, who were mostly from sub-Saharan Africa and had resided in France for quite some time, occupied the St. Bernard de la Chapelle church in Paris. Among the immigrants, ten men went on a hunger strike to force the French government to allow them to remain in the country. Jean-Louis Debré vowed not to give in. "I am determined, too," Debré declared (Whitney 1996:13). In late August, police in riot gear stormed the church and took more than 200 immigrants to a detention center. President Chirac defended these actions, asserting that France needed to send a strong signal to would-be illegal immigrants that they would not be tolerated. However, magistrates ruled that the police had improperly prepared warrants for the illegal immigrants, and the immigrants were thus released from custody.

The National Front, meanwhile, became an increasingly important player in French immigration politics. The move back to single-member, winner-take-all districts after the 1986 elections had harmed the FN's prospects in national elections, but the FN had nonetheless pulled all the major parties to the right on immigration issues. Indeed, their denouncement of the FN notwithstanding, the mainstream right parties adopted rhetoric similar to that of the FN, and the RPR-UDF coalition enacted policies that the FN and its supporters viewed as necessary and proper, even if they did not go far enough. Furthermore, in local elections, Le Pen's followers did quite well. In February 1997, the FN won control of the municipal council of the Marseilles suburb of Vitrolles. Bruno Mégret, an FN leader, was ineligible to run for the mayoral seat due to the fact that he had violated campaign spending laws in 1995, but his wife was able to win the office on his behalf. The FN had already won control of the local governments in Marignane, Orange, and Toulon, but Vitrolles was the first place where the FN won an absolute majority, since the other town offices had been won with several parties splitting the vote.

At the national level, the RPR-UDF government pushed for even stricter controls on immigrants. One law required French citizens to report the movements of visiting foreigners to the authorities. Exempt from this surveillance were visitors from wealthy nations in Europe, as well as from the United States and Japan. Many leading figures of the French intelligentsia—including actors, film directors, writers, musicians, lawyers, and scientists—spoke out vigorously against the policy, comparing it to measures enacted by the collaborationist Vichy regime that required the French to inform authorities about the movement of Jews. Prime Minister Alain Juppé defended the law, claiming it would help the state "tackle the very real network of illegal immigration that exists in France" (Simons 1997b:A6). Before the bill was passed, the European Parliament called on France to withdraw it from consideration. Juppé lashed out against the European Parliament, and the policy was enacted.

CONCLUSION

In 1997 Jacques Chirac called for new parliamentary elections a year before he was constitutionally required to do so. This turned out to be a horrific miscalculation for his political coalition. The Socialists, supported by the Green Parties and the PCF, and led by Lionel Jospin, went on to a resounding victory. Prime Minister Jospin's government moved immediately to ease what his party perceived to be some of the harshest aspects of France's immigration policies passed by the UPF, especially rapid deportations. Trade unions, civil rights organizations, and religious leaders supported the measures (Simons 1997a:A13). The Socialist government passed legislation in November 1997 that once again attributed French citizenship to children born in France of immigrant parents once they turned eighteen years old.

Meanwhile, the mainstream right fell into disarray when political leaders made deals with the National Front in order to win regional elections in 1998. President Chirac denounced such deals, and warned of the dangers of granting legitimacy and power to the far-right FN. Labor unions, religious leaders, and parties of the left led tens of thousands of people who took to the streets to protest the power-sharing deals. The FN clearly enjoyed the havoc it had sown within the mainstream right, going so far as to reelect against his will a regional executive who had resigned after coming to office with the help of FN votes. But the FN could not gloat too long, as divisions within its own ranks led to the ouster of Bruno Mégret, perhaps the best known of FN leaders after Le Pen himself.

Over the final two decades of the twentieth century, French immigration politics was radically transformed. Immigration ceased to be a technical issue and emerged as a highly charged point of political contention. With immigrant entries all but terminated already, political debates and public policies focused primarily on issues concerning France's existing immigrant population and their offspring. The statist tradition of an autonomous, unitary governmental apparatus seemed to fall asunder as presidents denounced the immigration policies of prime ministers and their cabinets, and as courts overturned laws enacted by parliament. Institutional changes mandated by a newly assertive judiciary eliminated the administrative and executive style of immigration policy-making, and forced decisions to be made in the far more contentious parliamentary arena. Immigration became an object of party competition and ideological manipulation. Short-lived institutional changes in France's voting laws helped propel the previously marginal National Front into the limelight. The FN in turn shaped public discourse in such a way that mainstream parties of the right and the left felt compelled or freed, depending on one's view, to take much tougher stands vis-à-vis immigration.

The full extent of this transformation is difficult to gauge. With the unemployment rate above 12 percent in the last few years of the century, we simply do not know at this point whether heightened labor demand in the future might once again lead France to encourage large-scale immigration. Immigrant organizations, though much more numerous and powerful than they were before 1981, are nonetheless not an important voice in the formulation of entry policy as they are in the United States, at least not yet. It does seem that it will be very difficult to put the genie back in the bottle in many respects. A return to an administrative and executive approach that treats immigration as a technical issue appears highly unlikely. A more fractured state characterized by parliamentary debate, judicial action, and party competition will most likely shape future immigration policy-making. If this is true, French immigration policy should be far less predictable in the years to come.

IV

CONCLUSION

Chapter 8

Immigration Policies in
Comparative Perspective

Taken together, the histories of French and U.S. immigration policies offer a telling portrait of modern immigration policies and the political processes through which such policies are made in advanced industrialized nations. These two liberal democracies enjoyed considerable economic prosperity in the second half of the twentieth century, and the economic opportunities available in these countries, combined with the political freedoms and relative social stability prevalent in their territories, rendered both France and the United States major destinations for immigrants throughout the globe. But at critical historical junctures, France and the United States implemented very different immigrant entry policies. In this study, I have suggested that political institutions played an important role in shaping immigration policies in these two nations. In this final chapter, I explicitly compare the two cases and make inferences based on the evidence presented throughout this book in an attempt to understand the considerable variation in immigration policy outcomes that we have observed. I then examine the implications of this study for the theoretical literature on immigration policies.

Perhaps the most glaring institutional difference we have seen between the United States and France, as it concerns immigration policy, lies in the relative cohesiveness of these nations' respective state apparatuses. The United States possesses a divided, fractious governmental system in this policy area. The executive and legislative branches have fought over entry policies, the two legislative chambers have fought over entry policies, the independent judiciary has stepped into the fray, and separate state governments have taken on the federal government. France, on the other hand, possesses a relatively unitary state. During the Fourth Republic (1946–1958), France's institutional arrangements fused powers and rendered parliament and its leadership supreme. There was little in the way of an independent judiciary to challenge parliamentary authority, and sub-national governments had no constitutional standing to challenge the central government. As a matter of course there were debates among state elites over immigration laws, but once the governing majority decided on a policy direction, opponents had few institutional mechanisms to challenge it. With the advent of the Fifth Republic in 1958, executive and legislative powers were supposedly separated, but without a presidential veto the state has remained very unitary. On the other hand, the French judiciary has gained some degree of independence over the last quarter century, and this has fractured the state somewhat.

Another prominent institutional difference we have seen between the two countries revolves around the extent to which various societal groups have been granted access to and influence over the immigration policy-making process. U.S. pluralist institutional structures have allowed a wide array of organized groups and individuals to participate in the making of immigrant entry laws. The French state, by contrast, has acted far more autonomously. Independent, nonstate associations have been suppressed for much of French history, and interests such as ethnic associations, patriotic societies, religious groups, and civil rights organizations have not been allowed to influence immigration policies in significant ways. Only employer groups and labor organizations have held any sway over French entry policies, and even the participation of these two powerful interests has been intermittent and often *post facto*.

The institutional divergence between these two countries in terms of their state structures partially accounts for the different immigrant entry policies that the United States and France have formulated and implemented. The evidence examined in this volume does not support, and indeed argues against, any notion of institutional determinism. Nonetheless, a close reading of the historical narrative does suggest that institutional structures have shaped immigration policy processes and outcomes in a causally significant manner. As noted earlier, the historical periodization of this book is designed with comparative intent, and thus Chapter 2 can be read in conjunction with Chapter 5, Chapter 3 with Chapter 6, and Chapter 4 with Chapter 7. By way of conclusion, let me draw out more explicitly some comparative lessons from these narratives.

Coming out of World War II, the United States and France confronted conditions relevant to immigration policy that were at once similar and different. Both faced labor shortages and both had long traditions of recruiting foreign workers to satisfy such needs. In France, wartime destruction rendered economic renewal a political priority, and a largely unitary and autonomous state embarked on an aggressive program of immigrant recruitment. Trade unions came to strongly oppose these liberal entry policies, and public opinion was also aligned heavily against immigration. But the unitary nature of French institutions denied opponents of immigration any sort of foothold within the state apparatus, and the government's relative autonomy prevented organized interests in civil society from having much influence over France's entry policies. Among those opposed to immigration, only organized labor enjoyed any sway over immigration policies, and its opposition was more than offset by support from business interests for mass labor migration. The state's relative autonomy insulated government elites and encouraged them to view immigration as a largely technical economic issue. Given France's labor needs, political elites opted for large-scale immigrant recruitment policies, and French institutional arrangements allowed these elites to implement such policies in an administrative and executive manner.

The United States also experienced heightened labor demand after the war, but proponents of liberal immigration policies were motivated as much, if not more, by their rejection of the racial and ethnic discrimination that underpinned the country's restrictive entry policies. The Truman administration set out to dismantle the discriminatory National Origins Quota System. However, U.S. political institutions ensured that this would be a highly charged political issue, and the fractured nature of the state provided opponents of such reforms with the means to defeat Truman's initiatives. Those who supported the National Origins Quota System were able to muster a two-thirds majority in Congress and perpetuate immigration restrictions based on race and ethnicity. U.S. pluralist institutions allowed a great many organized interests to participate in the policy-making process, and patriotic societies played a particularly important role in lobbying in favor of restrictive, discriminatory immigration quotas. It was not until 1965 that proponents of liberal and more egalitarian policies were able to gain control of the various branches of the fractured state and to repeal the National Origins Quota System.

By the late 1960s both France and the United States were receiving hundreds of thousands of legal immigrants per year. But the world economic crisis of the 1970s forced political elites to reconsider their entry policies. In France, the unitary and autonomous nature of the state allowed for relatively decisive action, and in 1974 the government suspended immigration. Once again, France's cohesive state structures prevented opponents of restrictive measures from securing any independent institutional power base from which to oppose the immigration ban. The French judiciary did assert some independence by overturning particular aspects of the immigration stoppage, but the government was nonetheless able to implement its restrictions. Organized societal interests were largely excluded from the decision-making process. Employers did have some degree of access to decision-makers, but their opposition to immigration restrictions was offset by the support offered by organized labor. Overall, insulated public officials saw the immigration stoppage as a rational, technical response to emerging economic conditions. French institutional structures fostered these views and allowed state elites to act accordingly.

Confronting similar economic difficulties, the Nixon administration and several Congressional leaders also sought to limit immigration. In the United States, political elites focused on ways to curtail illegal immigration in order to protect American workers, as well as legal immigrants, during this period of rising unemployment rates. To curb illegal immigration, political elites settled on a strategy of fining employers who knowingly hired undocumented aliens. U.S. political institutions allowed many organized groups in civil society to participate in the policy-making process. Agricultural employers, Hispanic organizations, and civil rights groups all fought against the proposed employer sanctions. The fractured nature of the state allowed those who opposed restrictions to gain an institutional power base in the Senate, particularly in that chamber's Subcommittee on Immigration and Naturalization. From this vantage point those who were opposed to employer sanctions were able to block such proposals throughout the 1970s. In the end, the divided and open nature of U.S. political institutions essentially negated the impact of prevailing economic conditions on immigration policy outcomes.

Thus, from the end of the war through the 1970s French and U.S. political institutions shaped power struggles over immigration policy quite differently and produced divergent policy outcomes. France's unitary and relatively autonomous state was able to take more decisive action. State elites were insulated from public pressures, and decisions concerning immigration policy were made outside the parliamentary arena. Decision-makers viewed immigration policy as a predominantly technical, economic issue. Employers and trade unions were powerful enough to make their voices heard, but because the former almost uniformly favored liberal policies and the latter called consistently for restrictions, these two economic interests offset each other to a large extent, affording the state a relatively free hand. The fact that societal influence was largely limited to these two class-based interests helped to frame immigration issues in almost exclusively economic terms. Government officials, operating in a technical, depoliticized context, opted for liberal policies during periods of economic prosperity and restrictive policies during hard times, leading to a strong correlation between immigration policies and economic conditions, particularly unemployment rates.

The United States, on the other hand, had a fractured and open institutional system, rendering decisive action difficult. Divided, pluralistic institutions tended to politicize immigration issues. In addition to employers and trade unions, noneconomic interests such as patriotic associations, ethnic groups, and civil liberties organizations were able to participate in the decision-making process; and consequently immigration was not framed in exclusively economic terms. The fractured nature of the state provided opponents of liberal and restrictive measures alike with institutional power bases from which to thwart policy initiatives. With numerous political elites operating from their own independent bases of power and with so many societal interests participating in the decision-making process, immigration policy outcomes were unpredictable and any correlation between entry policies and economic conditions was negated.

In the 1980s and 1990s U.S. institutional arrangements continued to divide the state and provide access to a wide array of interests. Economic conditions improved markedly by the mid-1980s, and the country embarked on a prosperous period characterized by high levels of growth and low rates of unemployment. With few interruptions, this remarkable expansion continued up to the end of the twentieth century. But several influential lawmakers continued to press for restrictive immigration measures in Congress. The reform efforts of the 1980s continued to focus on illegal immigration and the use of employer sanctions as a means to curtail undocumented entries. In light of improved economic conditions, proponents of these sanctions now presented them more as a "law-and-order" issue than an economic one. Once again, the fractured nature of the state made implementing such reforms an arduous task. Those who supported employer sanctions bundled them together with a generous amnesty provision for illegal aliens already residing in the United States. In a fractured institutional system that allows a wide spectrum of interests to participate in the decision-making process, such creative lawmaking was critical. The sanctions won over many in the labor movement, while the amnesty persuaded numerous ethnic organizations and civil rights groups to back the measure. By making it relatively easy to comply with the new prohibition on hiring undocumented aliens, congressional leaders were able to win over business interests as well, and the Immigration Reform and Control Act was passed in 1986.

In the 1990s immigration to the United States increased steadily. As the country's economic expansion gained momentum, the United States became as attractive a destination as ever. Entry policies that placed no limit on the number of immigrants who could come to reunite with close family members allowed chain migration in particular to accelerate. In 1994 the Republican Party, which had become increasing anti-immigration, gained control of both chambers of Congress. Political elites once again engaged in a bundling strategy, this time combining popular measures to combat illegal entries and to limit immigrants' access to public services with less popular measures to reduce legal immigration quotas for both economic and family immigration. The Republican leadership not only had majorities in both houses, but the cautious support of President Clinton for their initiative as well. However, there were many societal interests opposed to the proposed restrictions, and U.S. political institutions granted them considerable access to the policy-making process. Business organizations, ethnic associations, and trade unions led the charge against the proposed restrictions. In the end, reductions in legal immigration were defeated, and only measures to curb illegal entries at the nation's borders and measures that denied certain public benefits to immigrants were passed.

In France, meanwhile, economic difficulties were harder to overcome. Unemployment continued to rise throughout the 1980s and 1990s. Consequently, the French state maintained its prohibition on most immigrant entries during this period. Trade unions and even business leaders supported the nation's closed border policies. But while France's entry policies remained relatively stable, the politics of immigration underwent radical change. The judiciary's ruling that making immigration policies by administrative decree was unconstitutional had pushed the issue of immigration into parliament and politicized it. Mitterrand's decision to grant associational rights to foreigners allowed immigrants to organize, with the potential, so far largely unfulfilled, for such immigrant groups to influence immigration laws. Perhaps most importantly, the previously marginal National Front became an important force in the politics of immigration. These developments erased the ability of state elites to treat immigration policy as a technical issue. With the widespread consensus favoring restrictive immigrant entry policies, most debates over the last twenty years have focused on policies governing those already residing in France. However, employment conditions seem to be improving at the start of the new century, and some employers have begun calling for a limited liberalization of France's entry laws. It remains to be seen whether the institutional and political changes over the past two decades might alter the dynamics of immigration policy-making in France enough to end the strong relationship between entry policies and economic conditions that prevailed in the second half of the twentieth century.

This comparative study of French and U.S. immigration policies suggests that economic and cultural conditions cannot by themselves or in conjunction with one another adequately explain immigration policy outcomes in advanced industrialized nations. Instead, we must look at the important role played by political institutions in determining a nation's immigrant entry laws. A state's immigration laws result from policy-making processes that are structured and constrained by political institutions. Macro-level factors should be seen as potential and indirect influences on immigrant entry policies. Political institutions, and the human interactions they structure, determine which, if any, macro-level conditions will influence immigration policy outcomes.

There is a burgeoning body of literature in political science that contends institutional structures shape immigration policies, and the findings of *The*

Ramparts of Nations largely substantiate such claims. Nonetheless, there is little consensus on how institutions shape immigrant entry policies. In the literature, what we might broadly term "institutional" approaches vary widely. Jeannette Money's *Fences and Neighbors* argues that immigration issues are placed on the national agenda only when liberal or restrictionist constituencies can swing national election outcomes. Immigrants are geographically concentrated in host states, and thus political pressure to address immigration issues comes from a few localities that experience the preponderance of costs and benefits associated with immigration. Only when these specific localities are critical to national elections are immigration issues tackled in national legislatures. Societal pressures come from regions with large immigrant populations, and these pressures are channeled through a nation's political institutions to produce policy outcomes.

The historical narratives presented in *The Ramparts of Nations* offer certain caveats to Money's findings. We have indeed observed that politicians in the United States from states with large immigrant populations—such as California, New York, New Jersey, Texas, and Florida—are often active in the struggles over immigration policies. However, there is also a great deal of political entrepreneurship on the part of politicians who do not come from immigrant-rich states. In recent years no legislator has been more active in formulating immigration policy in the United States than Alan Simpson (R-WY), who represented a state with relatively few immigrants. Politicians such as Ted Kennedy (D-MA), James Eastland (D-MS), and Spencer Abrams (R-MI) have also taken the lead on immigration issues at critical historical junctures. Thus, while immigration is somewhat concentrated, it is apparent from the U.S. case that legislative leadership and activity on immigration issues is rather widespread. Furthermore, in those districts in the United States where there are large immigrant populations, it is impossible to predict what influence that situation will have on the positions taken by congressional representatives. Some like Peter Rodino (D-NJ) have taken restrictive positions, such as the call for employer sanctions, which are designed to protect the working population within their districts from immigrant competition. Others like Leon Panetta (D-CA) have taken liberal positions, such as support of guestworker programs, which are intended to guarantee that employers in their districts have access to immigrant labor. All told, immigrant concentration in particular electoral regions does not necessarily tell us where leadership and activity on immigration questions will come from or whether representatives from immigrant-rich areas will support liberal or restrictive policies. These considerations should inform any future exploration of the relationships among societal pressures, electoral institutions, and immigration policy outcomes.

James F. Hollifield's *Immigrants, Markets, and States* offers an argument about immigration and immigration policies that combines economic, cultural, and institutional considerations. Hollifield contends that increased economic interactions in the international arena have increased migratory pressures, while at the same time the rise of rights-based politics in liberal democracies has limited such nations' abilities to restrict immigrant entries. The result has been ever higher levels of immigration to advanced industrialized countries. Part of the institutional slant of Hollifield's argument is that civil rights, such as the rights to asylum and to family reunion, have been codified and are enforced by judiciary bodies, giving these nations an institutional bias toward liberal entry policies.

We have seen that in both France and the United States pro-immigration groups have indeed fought on behalf of the rights of immigrants, and that the rights to asylum and family reunion have presented obstacles to those wishing to curtail entries. However, these two historical narratives also belie the notion that institutionalized rights have prevented states from implementing far-reaching restrictions on immigration. The French case poses the most significant challenges to Hollifield's claims. We have seen that, over the course of the 1970s, France reduced legal labor migration by a staggering total of almost 90 percent. This is not to say that there were no institutional obstacles to French immigration restrictions in the 1970s. Most notably, the judiciary ruled that certain measures which aimed to restrict family immigration were illegal. But the French government was able to reformulate its restrictions on family immigration to comply with the court's ruling. Over the course of the 1970s, immigration for the purposes of family reunion was reduced by 50 percent. Institutionalized liberalism in France and elsewhere might protect family immigration more than it does labor immigration, but such institutional arrangements do not seem to prevent governments from enacting sweeping restrictions on immigrant entries.

Gary Freeman's 1995 article entitled "Modes of Immigration Politics in Liberal Democratic States" offers a political economy model of entry policies based on nations' institutional structures. Freeman reasons that in liberal democracies the general public is rationally ignorant about immigration. As a result, organized interests dominate immigration politics. Beneficiaries of immigration, particularly employers, are better placed to organize than are the workers who must compete with foreign labor and thus suffer the costs of immigration. In the end, organized business interests hold more sway over public officials than does the unorganized general opposition, and democracies thus lean toward more liberal entry policies.

The French and U.S. cases substantiate Freeman's claim that institutions shape political struggles among actors in ways that influences immigration policy outcomes. We have seen that these two liberal democratic states have indeed largely ignored general public opinion, and that only organized interests have been able to participate in the immigration policy-making process. However, the findings presented here demonstrate that restrictive forces, not just pro-immigration employers, have been able to organize effectively. Patriotic associations and trade unions in the United States were able to lobby successfully for the implementation and maintenance of the restrictive National Origins Quota System for much of the twentieth century. And in France a strong state, with the support of organized labor, was able to withstand employer pressure and implement the immigration stoppage of 1974.

Patrick Ireland's *The Policy Challenge of Ethnic Diversity* examines the ways in which institutional structures in host societies shape immigrant political mobilization. More than ethnicity or class, according to Ireland, institutional structures determine what forms immigration political behavior takes. In certain respects, Ireland's study is far different from *The Ramparts of Nations*. Ireland concentrates his efforts on incorporation policy, while this book focuses on entry policy. Ireland looks primarily at local policies, while this study concerns itself with national policy. Ireland analyzes the policy-making process, while this study looks first and foremost at outcomes. Nonetheless, *The Ramparts of Nations* reaffirms many of Ireland's findings and expands upon them. Most importantly, this study concurs with Ireland that whether institutional structures are open or closed plays a critical role in determining who can participate in the policy-making process and what forms participation may take. This book takes such claims one step further and suggests that, by shaping political interactions, institutional arrangements influence policy outcomes.

The works of Money, Hollifield, Freeman, Ireland, and others grow out of an emerging realization in the social sciences that institutions are more than merely formal arrangements; they are important determinants of political behavior and policy outcomes. *The Ramparts of Nations* builds on this tradition and offers a comparative and historical study illustrating that institutional arrangements are critical in determining immigrant entry policies. Future research should build further on such insights and develop broad comparative frameworks in order to better understand international migration policies that so profoundly influence the fates of nations and individuals alike.

Bibliography

"Avis adopté par le Conseil économique et social au cours de sa séance du 26 février 1969 sur le problème des travailleurs étrangers." (1969). *Journal Officiel de la République Française: Avis et Rapports du Conseil Économique et Social*, no.7. Paris: 321–324.

Bennett, David H. (1990). *The Party of Fear: From Nativist Movements to the New Right in American History*. New York: Vintage.

Bennett, M. T. (1966). "The Immigration and Nationality (McCarran-Walter) Act of 1952, as Amended to 1965." *The Annals of the American Academy of Political and Social Science* (September): 127–136.

Benoît, Jean. (1980). *Dossier E . . . comme Esclaves*. Paris: Editions Alain Moreau.

———. (1974). "Pour préparer une nouvelle politique l'entrée des immigrés est suspendue." *Le Monde*, July 5: 1, 24.

———. (1973). "M. Gorse propose une concertation permanente avec le patronat et les syndicats." *Le Monde*, May 10: 1, 36.

Bentley, Arthur F. (1908). *The Process of Government*. Chicago, IL: University of Chicago Press.

Beriss, David. (1990). "Scarves, Schools, and Segregation: The Foulard Affair." *French Politics & Society*, vol. 8, no. 1:1–13.

Briggs, V. M., Jr. (1984). *Immigration Policy and the American Labor Force*. Baltimore, MD: The Johns Hopkins University Press.

Brubaker, Rogers. (1992). *Citizenship and Nationhood in France and Germany*. Cambridge, MA: Cambridge University Press.

Calame, Paulette, and Pierre Calame. (1972). *Les Travailleurs étrangers en France*. Paris: Les Editions Ouvrières.

Calavita, Kitty. (1994). "U.S. Immigration Policy Responses: The Limits of Legislation." In Wayne A. Cornelius, Philip L. Martin and James F. Hollifield (eds.), *Controlling Immigration: A Global Perspective*. Stanford, CA: Stanford University Press.

Calvez, Corentin. (1969). "Le Problème des travailleurs étrangers." *Journal Officiel de la République Française: Avis et Rapports du Conseil Économique et Social*, no. 7. Paris: 308–320.

Carter, Jimmy. (1980). "Carter Legislative Message to Congress." *CQ Weekly Report*. January 26: 203–229.

Castells, Manuel. (1975). "Immigrant Workers and Class Struggles in Advanced Capitalism: The Western European Experience." *Politics and Society*, vol. 5: 33–66.

Castles, Stephen, and Godula Kosack. (1973). *Immigrant Workers and Class Structure in Western Europe*. New York: Oxford University Press.

Castles, Stephen, and Mark Miller. (1993). *The Age of Migration: International Population Movements in the Modern World*. London: Macmillan.

CCIP (Chambre de Commerce de Paris). (1957). "Mesures tendant à favoriser l'entrée en France de travailleurs étrangers." *Bulletin de la Chambre de Commerce de Paris* no. 4.

CEDETIM (Centre d'études anti-impérialistes). (1975). *Les immigrés: Contribution à l'histoire politique de l'immigration en France*. Paris: Édition Stock.

CGT (Confédération Générale du Travail). (1972). *XXXVIII Congrès National: Compte rendu in extenso des débats*. Paris: CGT.

———. (1967). *XXXVI Congrès National: Compte rendu in extenso des débats*. Paris: CGT.

———. (1963). *XXXIV Congrès National: Compte rendu in extenso des débats*. Paris: CGT.

———. (1948). *XXVII Congrès National de Paris: Compte rendu sténographié des débats*. Paris: CGT.

Chemillier-Gendreau, Monique. (1998). *L'injustifiable: Les politiques françaises de l'immigration*. Paris: Bayard Éditions.

Cheng, L., and E. Bonacich. (1984). *Labour Immigration Under Capitalism: Asian Workers in the United States Before World War II*. Berkeley, CA: University of California Press.

CNPF (Conseil National du Patronat Français). (1956). *Bulletin du CNPF* 150 (August).

Commissariat Général du Plan. (1971). *Rapport de la Commission: Emploi* (tome II). Paris: La Documentation française.

CQ *(Congressional Quarterly) Almanac*. Various years. Washington, DC: Congressional Quarterly Press.

Crozier, M. (1964). *The Bureaucratic Phenomenon*. Chicago: The University of Chicago Press.

Debré, Robert, and Alfred Sauvy (1946). *Des français pour la France*. Paris: Gallimard.

Dionne, E. J., Jr. (1983). "France and Aliens in Its Midst: Fear on Both Sides." *New York Times*. August 15: A2.

Dunlavy, Colleen A. (1993). *Political Structure and Industrial Change: Early Railroads in the United States and Prussia*. Princeton, NJ: Princeton University Press.

Eschbach, Karl, Jacqueline Hagan, Nestor Rodriguez, Rubén Hernández, and Stanley Bailey. (1999). "Death at the Border." *International Migration Review*, vol. 33, no. 2:430–454.

Felton, John. (1979). "Congress Receptive to Appeals to Increase Aid for Refugees." *CQ Weekly Report.* July 28: 1545–1546.

Finegold, Kenneth, and Theda Skocpol. (1995). *State and Party in America's New Deal.* Madison, WI: University of Wisconsin Press.

Fourastié, Jean. (1979). *Les Trente Glorieuses: La révolution invisible de 1946 à 1975.* Paris: Fayard.

Fragomen, Austin T., Jr. (1977). "1976 Amendments to Immigration & Nationality Act." *International Migration Review*, vol. 11, no.1: 95–100.

Freeman, Gary P. (1995). "Modes of Immigration Politics in Liberal Democratic States."*International Migration Review*, vol. 29, no. 4: 881–902.

———. (1979). *Immigrant Labour and Racial Conflict in Industrial Societies: The French and British Experience, 1945–1975.* Princeton, NJ: Princeton University Press.

Gani, Léon. (1972). *Syndicats et travailleurs immigrés.* Paris: Les Editions sociales.

Garson, J. P. (1986). *Migration clandestines, régularisations et marche du travail en France: Contrainte nationals et internationals.* Geneva: International Labor Organization.

Gimpel, J. G., and J. R. Edwards, Jr. (1999). *The Congressional Politics of Immigration Reform.* Boston, MA: Allyn and Bacon.

Hall, Peter A. (1990). "Pluralism and Pressure Politics." In Peter A. Hall et al. (eds.), *Developments in French Politics.* New York: St. Martin's Press.

———. (1986). *Governing the Economy: The Politics of State Intervention in Britain and France.* New York: Oxford University Press.

Hammar, Tomas. (1985). *European Immigration Policy: A Comparative Study.* Cambridge, UK: Cambridge University Press.

Haus, Leah. (1999). "Labor Unions and Immigration Policy in France." *International Migration Review*, vol. 33, no. 3: 683–716.

Henneresse, Marie-Claude. (1979). *Le patronat et la politique française d'immigration, 1945–1975.* Thèse de troisième cycle, Paris: Institut d'études politiques.

Herbert, Ulich. (1990). *A History of Foreign Labour in Germany, 1880–1980.* Ann Arbor, MI: The University of Michigan Press.

Higham, John. (1955). *Strangers in the Land: Patterns of American Nativism, 1860–1925.* New Brunswick, NJ: Rutgers University Press.

Hohl, Donald G. (1976). "Attempts at Immigration Reform: 94th Congress." *International Migration Review*, vol. 10, no. 4: 523–525.

———. (1975). "US Immigration Legislation—Prospects in the 94th Congress." *International Migration Review*, vol. 9, no. 1: 59–62.

———. (1974). "Proposed Revisions of U.S. Western Hemisphere Immigration Policies." *International Migration Review*, vol. 8, no. 1: 69–76.

Hohl, Donald G., and Michael G. Wenk. (1973). "The Illegal Alien and the Western Hemisphere Immigration Dilemma." *International Migration Review*, vol. 7, no. 3: 323–332.

———. (1971). "Current U.S. Immigration Legislation: Analysis and Comment." *International Migration Review*, vol. 5, no. 3: 339–356.

Hollifield, James F. (1992). *Immigrants, Markets, and States: The Political Economy of Postwar Europe*. Cambridge, MA: Harvard University Press.

Hucker, Charles W. (1979). "Carter Refugee Legislation Raises Fundamental Policy Questions for the Congress." *CQ Weekly Report* (June 2).

Husbands, Christopher T. (1991). "The Mainstream Right and the Politics of Immigration in France: Developments in the 1980s." *Ethnic and Racial Studies*, vol. 14, no. 2: 170–198.

Ibrahim, Youssef M. (1994). "France Bans Muslim Scarf In Its Schools." *New York Times*. September 11: 4.

———. (1990). "Bomb Destroys a French Mosque In Latest Display of Race Tension." *New York Times*. March 16: A2.

Idelson, Holly. (1995a). "House Panel Bill Cracks Down On Legal and Illegal Entry." *CQ Weekly Report*. July 15.

———. (1995b). "Immigration: Bridging Gap Between Ideas and Action." *CQ Weekly Report*. April 15: 1065–1071.

"Illegal Alien Employment." (1972). *CQ Weekly Report*. September 23: 2403.

IMF (International Monetary Fund). (1998). *International Financial Statistics Yearbook*. Washington, DC.

Immergut, Ellen M. (1992). *Health Politics: Interests and Institutions in Western Europe*. Cambridge, UK: Cambridge University Press.

INS (Immigration and Naturalization Service). (1999). *1997 Statistical Yearbook of the INS*. Washington, DC: U.S. Department of Justice.

———. (1997). *1996 Statistical Yearbook of the INS*. Washington, DC: U.S. Department of Justice.

Ireland, Patrick. (1994). *The Policy Challenge of Ethnic Diversity: Immigration Politics in France and Switzerland*. Cambridge, MA: Harvard University Press.

Katznelson, Ira. (1998). "The Doleful Dance of Politics and Policy: Can Historical Institutionalism Make a Difference?" *American Political Science Review*, vol. 92, no. 1: 191–197.

Kesselman, Mark, Joel Krieger, Christopher S. Allen, Stephen Hellman, David Ost, and George Ross. (1997). *European Politics in Transition*, 3rd Edition. New York: Houghton Mifflin Company.

Kindleberger, Charles P. (1967). *Europe's Postwar Growth: The Role of Labor Supply*. Cambridge, MA: Harvard University Press.

Koelble, Thomas A. (1995). "The New Institutionalism in Political Science." *Comparative Politics*, vol. 27: 231–243.

LeMay, Michael C. (1989). "U.S. Immigration Policy and Politics." In Michael C. LeMay (ed.), *The Gatekeepers: Comparative Immigration Policy*. New York: Praeger.

———. (1987). *From Open Door to Dutch Door: An Analysis of U.S. Immigration Policy Since 1820*. Westport, CT: Praeger.

"Les reactions en France." (1974). *Le Monde*, July 6: 24.

"Les travailleurs étrangers en France." (1972). *Economie Géographie* no. 95:1–9.

"Les travailleurs étrangers en France." (1972). *Notes et Arguments* no. 26.

Levi, M. (1988). *Of Rule and Revenue*. Berkeley, CA: University of California Press.

Lijphart, Arend, and Markus M.L. Crepaz. (1990). "Corporatism and Consensus

Democracy in Eighteen Countries: Conceptual and Empirical Linkages." *British Journal of Political Science*, vol. 21: 235–256.

Martin, Philip L. (1980). *Guestworker Programs: Lessons from Europe*. Washington, DC: U.S. Department of Labor.

Mauco, Georges. (1977). *Les Étrangers en France et le problème du racisme*. Paris: La Pensée Universelle.

Meissner, Doris. (1992). "Managing Migrations." *Foreign Policy*, vol. 86 (Spring): 66–83.

Miller, Harris N. (1985). "The Right Thing to Do: A History of Simpson-Mazzoli." In Nathan Glazer (ed.), *Clamor at the Gates: The New American Immigration*. San Francisco, CA: Institute for Contemporary Studies.

Miller, Mark J. (1981). *Foreign Workers in Western Europe: An Emerging Political Force*. New York: Praeger.

Minces, Juliette (1973). *Les Travailleurs étrangers en France*. Paris: Éditions du Seuil.

Ministère du Travail. (1976). *Le Dossier de l'immigration*. Paris.

Money, Jeannette. (1999). *Fences and Neighbors: The Political Geography of Immigration Control*. Ithaca, NY: Cornell University Press.

Montgomery, Paul L. (1972). "Illegal Aliens Here Called Public-Services Burden." *New York Times*. March 11: 58.

Moulier, Yann, and Georges Tapinos. (1979). "France." In Daniel Kubat (ed.), *The Politics of Migration Policies: The First World in the 1970s*. New York: The Center for Migration Studies of New York.

Noiriel, Gérard. (1988). *Le creuset français: Histoire de l'immigration, XIXe-XXe siècle*. Paris: Éditions du Seuil.

OECD (Organization for Economic Cooperation and Development). (1999). *Labour Forces Statistics, 1977–1997*. Paris: OECD.

———. (1984). *Labour Force Statistics, 1962–1982*. Paris: OECD.

OMI (Office de Migrations Internationales). (1994). *Omistats: Annuaire des Migrations*. Paris: Imprimerie Nationale.

ONI (Office National d'Immigration). (1974). *Statistiques de l'Immigration: Année 1974*. Paris: ONI.

Petras, Alizabeth McLean. (1981). "The Global Labour Market in the Modern World Economy." In M. M. Kritz et al. (eds.), *Global Trends in Migration*, New York: Center for Migration Studies.

Piore, M. J. (1979). *Birds of Passage: Migrant Labour in Industrial Societies*. Cambridge: Cambridge University Press.

Pizzorno, Alessandro. (1981). "Interests and parties in pluralism." In Suzanne Berger (ed.), *Organizing Interests in Western Europe: Pluralism, Corporatism, and the Transformation of Politics*. New York: Cambridge University Press.

Reimers, David M. (1992). *Still the Golden Door: The Third World Comes to America*. New York: Columbia University Press.

———. (1982). "Recent Immigration Policy: An Analysis." In Barry R. Chiswick (ed.), *The Gateway: U.S. Immigration Issues and Policies*. Washington, DC: American Enterprise Institute for Public Policy Research.

Riding, Alan. (1993a). "France Takes Tough Stance on Crime and Immigration." *New York Times*. April 9: A2.

———. (1993b). "French Parliament Approves Tighter Immigration Controls." *New York Times*. May 14: A8.

———. (1991a). "Immigrant Unrest Alarming French." *New York Times*. June 23: 9.

———. (1991b). "France Unveils Strict New Rules on Immigration." *New York Times*. July 11: A5.

———. (1990). "A Surge of Racism in France Brings a Search for Answers." *New York Times*. May 27: 1, 16.

Safran, William. (1998). *The French Polity*, 5th Edition. New York: Longman.

Sauvy, Alfred. (1946). "Evaluation des besoins de l'immigration française." *Population*, vol. 1:91–98.

Schain, Martin A. (1993). "Policy-making and defining ethnic minorities: the case of immigration in France." *New Community*, vol. 20, no. 1: 59–77.

———. (1990). "Immigration and Politics." In Peter A. Hall, Jack Hayward, and Howard Machin (eds.), *Developments in French Politics*. St. Martin's Press.

———. (1987). "The National Front and the Construction of Political Legitimacy." *West European Politics*, vol. 10, no. 2: 229–252.

Silverman, Maxim. (1992). *Deconstructing the Nation: Immigration, Racism, and Citizenship in Modern France*. New York: Routledge.

Simons, Marlise. (1997a). "French Socialists Say They'll Ease Up on Immigrant Crackdown." *New York Times*. June 12: A13.

———. (1997b). "Report Foreign Guests? French Tempers Flare." *New York Times*, February 20: A6.

Singer, Daniel. (1991). "The Resistible Rise of Jean-Marie Le Pen." *Ethnic and Racial Studies*, vol. 14, no. 3: 368–381.

Singer-Kérel, Jeanne (1991). "Foreign Workers in France, 1891–1936." *Ethnic and Racial Studies*, vol. 14: 279–293.

Skocpol, Theda. (1985). "Bringing the State Back In: Strategies of Analysis in Current Research." In Peter B. Evans, Dietrich Rueschemeyer, and Theda Skocpol (eds.), *Bringing The State Back In*. Cambridge, UK: Cambridge University Press.

Spencer, I. R. G. (1997). *British Immigration Policy Since 1939: The Making of a Multi-Racial Britain*. London: Routledge.

Spero, Joan E., and Jeffrey A. Hart. (1997). *The Politics of International Economic Relations*, 5th Edition. New York: St. Martin.

Steinmo, Sven, Kathleen Thelen, and Frank Longstreth. (1992). *Structuring Politics: Historical Institutionalism in Comparative Analysis*. Cambridge, UK: Cambridge University Press.

Taguieff, Pierre-André. (1985). "L'identité française et ses ennemis, le traitement de l'immigration dans le national-racisme français." *L'Homme et la societé* no. 3: 77–78.

Tapinos, Georges. (1975). *L'Immigration étrangère en France, 1946–1973*. Paris: Presses Universitaires de France.

Thelen, K., and S. Steinmo. (1992). "Historical institutionalism in comparative perspective." In S. Steinmo et al., *Structuring Politics: Historical Institutionalism in Comparative Analysis*. Cambridge, UK: Cambridge University Press.

Tichenor, D. J. (1994). "The Politics of Immigration Reform in the United States, 1981–1990." *Polity*, vol. 26, no. 3: 333–362.

"Transcript of the President's News Conference Emphasizing Domestic Matters." (1972). *New York Times*. June 23: 14.

Truman, David. (1951). *The Governmental Process*. New York: Knopf.

Ueda, Reed. (1994). *Postwar Immigrant America: A Social History*. New York: Bedford Books.

"Un mouvement de grève des travailleurs arabes a été diversement suivi." (1973). *Le Monde*, December 19:32.

U.S. Congress. (1973). *Illegal Aliens: A Review of Hearings Conducted During the 92nd Congress By Subcommittee No. 1 of the Committee on the Judiciary*. Washington, DC: U.S. Government Printing Office.

U.S. Department of Commerce. (1998). *Survey of Current Business*. Washington, DC: Bureau of Economic Analysis.

U.S. Department of Labor. (2001). *Consumer Price Index—All Urban Consumers, 1913–2000*. Washington, DC: Bureau of Labor Statistics.

Weil, Patrick. (1991). *La France et ses étrangers: l'aventure d'une politique de l'immigration, 1938–1991*. Paris: Calmann.

———. (1988). *L'analyse d'une politique publique: la politique française d'immigration, 1974–1988*. Thèse de cycle supérieur. Paris: Institut d'études politiques.

Whitney, Craig. (1996). "Paris Fight Over Aliens is Waged In a Church." *New York Times*. August 11: 13.

Wihtol de Wenden, Catherine. (1988). *Les immigrés et la politique: Cent cinquante ans d'évolution*. Paris: Presses de la Fondation Nationale des Sciences Politiques.

Wilson, Frank L. (1983). "Interest Groups and Politics in Western Europe: The Neo-Corporatist Approach." *Comparative Political Studies*, vol. 16 (October): 118–119.

Zolberg, Aristide R. (1990). "Reforming the Back Door: The Immigration Reform and Control Act of 1986 in Historical Perspective." In Virginia Yans-McLaughlin (ed.), *Immigration Reconsidered: History, Sociology, and Politics*. New York: Oxford University Press.

———. (1978). "International Migration Policies in a Changing World System." In William H. McNeill and Ruth S. Adams (eds.), *Human Migration: Patterns and Policies*. Bloomington: Indiana University Press.

Index

Abrams, Spencer, 141
Afghanistan, 31
African-Americans, 47, 56
Agricultural interests, 48–49, 65–67
Aid to Families with Dependent Children, 75
The Age of Migration, 3
Algeria, 85, 90, 94
Ali Djellali Ben, 100
American Business for Legal Immigration, 73
American Civil Liberties Union (ACLU), 73
American Coalition, 35
American Coalition of Patriotic Societies, 38
American Committee for Italian American Migration, 37
American Hellenic Educational Progressive Association (AHEPA), 37
American Immigration Lawyers Association, 73
American Legion, 35, 38
Amnesty, 64–65, 68
Anderson, Donald, 38
Arabia, 31

Arywitz, Sigmund, 47
Asiatic Barred Zone, 34, 41
Asiatic Exclusion League, 30
Association Law, 120
Auroux Laws, 121
Autain, François, 119

Badillo, Herman, 48
Balladur, Edouard, 129
Barre, Raymond, 112
Bayrou, François, 130
Belgium, 3
Berman, Howard, 74
Bideberry, Pierre, 88
Bidonvilles, 99–100
Biemiller, Andrew J., 38
Bonnechère, Michèle, 110
Bracero agreement, 33–34
Bracero program, 46
British treasury, 6
Brubaker, Rogers, 6–7
Buck, Pearl S., 34
Burlingame Treaty, 30
Burton, Sala, 65

California, 30–31, 72
California Supreme Court, 30

Calvez, Corentin, 101, 102, 103
Canada, 3, 52, 53
Capitalism, 4–5
Carey, James B., 38
Carter, Jimmy, 50, 54, 56, 62
Castles, Stephen, 114
Catholic immigrants, 29
CATO Institute, 73
Celler, Emanuel, 39
Chaban-Delmas, Jacques, 100
Chamber of Commerce, U.S., 64, 65, 68
Chamber of Commerce, Paris, 91
Chemillier-Gendreau, Monoque, 118
Cheysson, Claude, 120
China, 57
Chinese American Citizens Alliance, 36
Chinese Exclusion Act, 30, 34
Chinese immigrants, 41
Chirac, Jacques, 112, 120, 125, 126, 128, 130, 131, 132
Chotard, Yvon, 109
Citizens Committee to Repeal Chinese Exclusion, 34
Citroën, 94, 123
Civil libertarians, 65
Civil rights, 48, 58, 142
Civil War, 29
Clinton, Bill, 70, 74–75, 139–40
Coehlo, Tony, 64
Cold War, 34
Comité des Forges, 83
Comité des Houllères, 83
Commissariat Général du Plan, 89, 103–4
Commonwealth Immigrants Act, 6
Communism, 86
Confederation Française Démocratique du Travail (CFDT), 102, 106
Confédération Française des Travailleurs Chrétiens, 87
Confédération Générale du Travail, 83, 85, 86, 87, 102, 106, 110
Confédération National du Patronat Français (CNPF), 90, 91, 109
Congress, U.S.: Act to Encourage Immigration and, 29; Asiatic Barred Zone and, 31; Chinese immigration and, 30; employer sanctions and, 63–68; Hart-Celler Act and, 14, 27; illegal immigrants and, 47–51; Japanese immigration and, 31; Kennedy reforms and, 37; McCarran-Walter Act and, 27, 36; National Origins Quota System and, 32, 38; 1990s reforms and, 71–75; pluralist system, 15; post WWII policy and, 34; refugee policy and, 56, 57; Second Quota Act and, 31–32; universal entry policy and, 52–54
Conseil d'Etat, 111
Conseil National du Patronat Français, 104–5
Conseils des Prud'hommes, 121
Constitutional Council, 9, 122, 130
Consultative Assembly, 82
Contract Labor Act, 29–30
Cook, Marlow, 49
Council of Jewish Federations, 73
Council of Ministers, 98, 108, 110, 114–15, 120, 122, 126
Council of State, 130
Cresson, Edith, 128
Croizat, Ambroise, 81, 85, 86

Daughters of the American Revolution, 35, 38
Debré, Jean-Luis, 130
De Gaulle, Charles, 82
Democratic National Convention, 65
Désir, Harlem, 128
Diab, Mohamed, 100
Dijoud, Paul, 112
Dixecrats, 38
Dufoix, Georgina, 121–22
Dufriche, Marcel, 107
Durafour, Michel, 112

Eastland, James, 20, 49, 50, 53, 63, 141
Economic and Social Council, 16, 102
Eilberg, Joshua, 49, 53
Employer sanctions, 20–21, 61–62, 63–68, 138, 139
Ervin, Sam, 49
European Community, 122

European Economic Community, 9, 109, 113
European Parliament, 131
Evian Agreements, 94, 113

Federation for American Immigration Reform (FAIR), 72
Fédération Nationale des Syndicates d'Exploitants Agricoles, (FNSEA), 109
Fédération Nationale du Bâtiment (FNB), 93
Federation of Cleaning Enterprises, 109
Federation of Organized Trades and Labor Unions, 30
Fences and Neighbors, 141
Ferraro, Geraldine, 65
Filipino Federation of American, 36
Flores, Joseph, 48
Fong, Hiram, 49
Fontanet, Joseph, 104
Force Ouvrière (FO), 85, 102, 110
Ford, Gerald, 50, 54, 55–56
Foucault, Michel, 100
Fourastié, Jean, 79
France's immigration policy: Algerian immigrants and, 90; citizenship and, 126, 129; cohabitation period and, 125–26; Constitutional Council and, 130; corporatist dynamic and, 21; cultural influence on, 11; economic crisis and, 102, 108–9, 97–98; economic influence on, 5–6, 8, 18–19; employer management of, 83; ethnic screening and, 82–83, 85; executive control of, 80, 84; family reunification and, 122–23; forced departures and, 113, 119; hostility toward immigrants and, 100; housing adequacy and, 99–100; illegal immigrants and, 79, 86, 89–90, 92–93, 104–7, 119–20, 122, 128, 129, 30–31; immigration ban and, 108–13; immigration rate and, 3, 91–62, 99, 103; Jospin and, 131; La Haine and, 129–31; labor interests and, 85–87, 90–91; manpower camp and, 81–

82, 83; Marcelin-Fontanet circulars and, 104–7; National Front emergence and, 123–25; *Office National d'Immgiration* (ONI) and, 16, 84–89, 94; parliamentary involvement in, 113–14, 118; populationist camp and, 82–83; post WWII economy and, 79–80; racial tensions and, 127–28; refugee policy, 126; restrictive shift in, 21–22; Socialist regime and, 118–23, 131; State Council and, 113; statist-corporatist system of, 15–17; voluntary associations and 15–16; voluntary repatriation and, 112–13, 119, 123
Frank, Barney, 65
Freeman, Gary, 13, 142, 143
French Communist Party, 118, 124, 127

Gallegly, Elton, 72, 74
Genet, Jean, 100
Gentelmen's Agreement, 31
Germany, 6–7, 35
Germersheim, West Germany, 89
Gibbons, William J., 35
Gilman, Leonard, 48
Giscard d'Estaing, Valéry, 22, 108, 109, 118
The Good Earth, 34
Gonzalez, Henry, 66
Gorse, Georges, 107
Great Britain, 3, 6, 32, 35
Great Depression, 32
Greece, 32, 189
Green Parties, 131

Habitation à Loyer Modéré (HLM), 99
Hall, Peter, 17
Hannoun, Michel, 126
Hart, Philip, 39
Hart-Celler Act of 1965, 14, 20, 36–39, 40, 45, 52, 68
Hawaiian Islands, 31
Hayes, Rutherford B., 30, 41
Helms, Jesse, 73
Hernandez, Antonia, 64
Hesburgh, Theodore, 70

Hesburgh Commission, 62
High Committee for Population, 82
Hispanic Caucus, 65
Hollifield, James F., 141–42, 143
Holtzman, Elizabeth, 56
House Subcommittee on Immigration
    and Nationality, 53
House Subcommittee on Immigration
    and Naturalization, 47, 49
Huang, John, 74
Humphrey, Hubert H., 35

Illegal Immigration Reform and Indi-
    vidual Responsibility Act, 70–75
*Immigrant Workers and Class Struc-
    ture in Western Europe,* 114
Immigrants, Markets, and States, 141–
    42
Immigration Act of 1965, 8, 20, 28,
    39, 45–46, 51
Immigration Act of 1990, 68–70, 75
Immigration and Nationality Act
    Amendments, 54
Immigration and Nationality Act, 36
Immigration and Naturalization Service
    (INS), 33, 46, 51
Immigration policy, 3–4; comparative
    research questions on, 7–9, 11; cul-
    tural influence on, 6–7; economic in-
    fluence on, 4–6, 7; government
    system and, 138–39; job competition
    and, 5; labor shortages and, 136–37.
    See also France's immigration policy;
    Political institutions; U.S. immigra-
    tion policy
Immigration Reform and Control Act
    of 1986, 20, 61, 62–68, 75
India, 31, 45
Ireland, 35
Ireland, Patrick, 143
Irish Immigration Reform Movement,
    68–69
Italy, 32, 86, 87, 89, 93

Japanese American Citizens League
    (JACL), 36, 37
Jeanneney, Jean-Marcel, 92
Johnson, Lyndon B., 38, 39, 40

Jordan, Barbara, 56, 70
Jordan Commission, 71
Jospin, Lionel, 1361
Joxe, Pierre, 127
Judd, Walter, 34, 36
Judiciary Committee, 34, 49
Juppé, Alain, 130, 131
Justice Department, 66

Kennedy, Edward M. (Ted), 52, 53,
    56, 69, 141
Kennedy, John F., 40
Kesselman, Mark, 103
Knights of Labor, 30
Know-Nothing Party, 71
Korea, 31, 45
Korean National Association, 36
Kosack, Godula, 114

Labor Department, 51
Latin America, 45
Le Chapelier law, 15–16
Le Pen, Jean-Marie, 118, 121, 124,
    125, 131
Lehman, Herbert H., 35
Lincoln, Abraham, 29
Lourraine Federation, 109
Lungren, Dan, 65–66
Lutheran Immigration Service, 37

McCarran, Patrick, 34, 35, 36
McCarran-Walter Act of 1952, 15, 28,
    37, 40
McClellan, John, 49
McCollum, Bill, 64
McCulloch, William, 52
McDermott, Jim, 74
Maghreb, 126
Marcellin, Raymond, 104
Marcellin-Fontanet circulars, 104–7
Marsellies Defense Committee, 101
Masaoka, Mike M., 37
Mauco, Georges, 82, 85
Mauroy, Pierre, 119, 120
Mazzoli, Romano, 63, 64, 66
Mégret, Bruno, 131, 132
Meissner, Doris, 6

Mexican American Legal Defense and Educational Fund, 69
Mexican immigrants, 32, 33–34
Mexico, 52, 53
Minister of Interior, 83, 113
Minister of National Solidarity, 119
Ministry of Labor, 83, 84, 90, 92, 93–94
Ministry of Population, 84
Ministry of Social Affairs, 102
Minjoz, Jean, 91
Mitterrand, Francois: Chirac and, 128; citizenship and, 126; foreign political organization and, 17, 22, 18, 140; illegal immigrants and, 120; immigrant associations and, 121; immigrant rights and, 120–21; National Assembly and, 125, 126; parliamentary changes and, 118–19; racism and, 127
"Modes of Immigration Politics in Liberal Democratic States," 142
Mondale, Walter, 66
Money, Jeannette, 13, 141, 143
Monnet, Jean, 81–82
Monnet Plan, 87
Morocco, 94

National Assembly, 17, 22, 98, 113, 118, 125, 126, 127
National Association for the Advancement of Colored People (NAACP), 47, 49, 51
National Catholic Rural Life Conference, 35
National Catholic Welfare Conference, 37
National Commission on Foreign Labor, 16, 107
National Council of Churches of Christ, 37
National Council of Jewish Women, 37
National Council of La Raza, 69, 73
National Employment Agency, 104
National Federation of Independent Business, 73

National Front (FN), 17, 22–23, 112, 118, 121, 123–25, 132
National Immigration Office, 81
National Institute for Population Studies, 82
National Labor Union (NLU), 29
National Lutheran Council, 38
National Origins Quota System: cultural influence on, 7; ethnic group organization and, 37, ethnic superiority and, 34–35, 27; Johnson and, 37 Kennedy and, 36–37; McCarran-Walter bill and, 34–36; political institutions and, 35; 1960s and, 8, 20; religious groups and, 37; repeal of, 39, 41, 137; Truman and, 15; World War II and, 33
A Nation of Immigrants, 36
Nazi Germany, 34
Netherlands, 3
New Order, 101
Nixon, Richard, 20, 47–48, 53, 138
Noiriel, Gerard, 11
Nonimmigrant nations, 6

Oakland, 30
Office Français de Protection des Réfugiés et Apatrides (OFPRA), 126
Office National d'Immgiration (ONI), 16, 84–89, 94
Oil crisis, 8, 108
O'Neal, Maston, 38
O'Neill, Thomas, 64, 66
Order of the Star Spangled Banner (OSSB), 29
Order of United Americans (OUA), 29
Organization of Chinese Americans, 69
Ortiz, Solomon, 66

Panetta, Leon, 65–66, 67, 141
Parisian Construction Federation, 105, 109
Pasqua, Charles, 126, 127, 129
Pasqua Law, 126, 127
Peugeot, 109, 123
Philippines, 45
Pilliod, Alva L., 48
Planning Commission, 82

Plyler v. Doe, 72–73
Poland, 32
The Policy Challenge of Ethnic Diversity, 143
Political institutions, 11–12; France-U.S. similarities and, 13–14; Freeman study and, 142; government systems and, 14–16, 135–36; Hollifield study and, 141–42; interests groups and, 14; political actor interaction and, 12; power relations and, 12, 14; public opinion and, 13–14; research on, 13; societal group differences and, 136; study results and, 140–41, 142–43. *See also* Trade unions
Political institutions (French): business/labor interests and, 79–81; government system changes and, 117–18; hostility toward immigrants and, 100–101; immigration accords and, 94; immigration restriction and, 98–99, 102–3, 109, 114–15; labor interests and, 85–87, 91; labor recruitment programs and, 93–94
Political institutions (U.S.): economic crisis and, 44; employer sanctions and, 61–62, 63–65, 65–66; fractured state and, 58–59; Immigration Act of 1990 and, 70; National Origins Quota System and, 28, 35; political actors and, 44–45; refugee policy and, 57; Simpson-Smith plan and, 73; sociocultural conditions and, 44. *See also* Congress, U.S.
Pompidou, Georges, 22, 100, 101, 104, 108
Portugal, 94
Postel-Vinay, André, 109
Proposition 187, 72

Questiaux, Nicole, 119

Rally for the Republic, 120
Reagan, Ronald, 62, 63, 67
Refugee Act, 57
Refugee policy, 54–57, 73, 126
Richardson, Bill, 66

Rifkind, Simon H., 35
Rocard, Michel, 126–27
Rodino, Peter, 49, 50, 52, 53, 56, 63, 67
Roosevelt, Theodore, 31, 33
Roybal, Edward R., 65

Samuel, Howard D., 47
San Francisco School Board, 30, 31
Sand Lot party, 30
Saoudi, Saad, 127
Sardinia, 93
Sartre, Jean-Paul, 100
Sauvy, Alfred, 82
Schumer, Chuck, 67
Schwartz, Abba, 36
Secretary of State for Immigrant Workers, 109
Secretary of State for Immigration, 119
Senate Subcommittee on Immigration and Naturalization, 20, 51, 59, 138
Sicily, 93
Simon, Paul, 70
Simpson, Alan, 63, 64, 65, 72, 141
Slavery, 12, 29
Smith, Lamar, 71, 72
Smith, Larry, 65
Smith, Virginia, 57
Smith Act, 33
Social Action Fund, 100
Société Générale d'Immigration, 83
S.O.S. Racism, 128
Spain, 94
State Council, 113
Stein, Daniel, 72
Stoléru, Lionel, 112
Supplemental Security Income, 75
Supreme Court of the United States, 30
Sweeney, John, 73
Switzerland, 4, 5
Sylla, Fodé, 129
Syndicat Agricoles, 83

Taft, William, 31
Talbot, 123
Thomas, Virginia, 68
Thurmond, Strom, 49
Taiwan, 45

Torres, Esteban, 66
Trade unions: corporatist constraints and, 91; employer sanctions and, 67; forced departures and, 113; illegal immigrants and, 46–47, 119–20; Marcellin-Fontanet circulars and, 105–7; National Origins Quota System and, 28; *Office National d' Immigration* (ONI) and, 84; policy reversal by, 38; recruitment support by, 86; restrictive stance by, 80, 110; voluntary repatriation and, 123
Truman, Harry S., 15, 28, 36, 40, 137
Tunisia, 94
Turkey, 94

Unemployment: Chirac and, 112; Cresson and, 128; economic crisis and, 97; employer sanctions and, 61, 63; illegal immigrants and, 46; immigration rate and, 103; increase of, comparison on, 9; 1980s decrease of, 68; 1980s increase of, 61, 63; 1990s and, 73; Nixon and, 48; oil crisis and, 108; Socialist regime and, 121
Union for French Democracy, 120
Union por la France du progress (UPF), 129–30, 131
U.S. Commission on Immigration Reform, 70
U.S. Constitution, 14, 15
U.S. Immigration Bureau, 29
U.S. immigration policy: anti-immigrant movements, 29; *bracero* program and, 46; Chinese migrants, 30 cultural influence on, 11, 58; depression era and, 32–33; economic crisis and, 43, 44; economic influence on, 6, 8, 19; employer sanctions and, 20–21, 47–51, 58–59, 63, 139; family reunification and, 39; federal system and, 14–15, 19; First

Quota Acts and 31–32; illegal immigrants and, 43–44, 46–51, 61–63, 71, 138, 139; Illegal Immigration Reform and Individual Responsibility Act and, 70–75; Immigration Act of 1965 and, 45–46; immigration Act of 1990 and, 68–70; immigration rate and, 3; Immigration Reform and Control Act and, 62–68; interest group, 14; Japanese immigrants and, 30–31, 33; job skills and, 37; Mexican farmhands immigrants and, 33–34; 1920's rate and, 32; pluralist dynamics and, 14; postwar economic expansion and, 27 pre-WWII and, 28–33; racial discrimination and, 34–35; refugee policy and, 54–57 skilled labor and, 69; trade unions and, 38 universal entry policy and, 51–54; unpredictability of, 19; World War II and, 33. *See also* Congress, U.S.; National Origins Quota System
U.S. Select Commission on Immigration and Refugee Policy, 62, 63
U.S. Supreme Court, 72–73

Vietnamese immigrants, 55–56
Villiers, Georges, 90
Vivien, André, 100
Voting rights, 120–21

Walter, Francis E., 34, 36
Watson, Barbara, 53
Welfare system, 48
West Germany, 3, 5
White, Richard, 48–50
Wilson, Charles, 57
Wilson, Pete, 65–66
Wilson, Woodrow, 31

Yee, Melinda, 69
Yugoslavia, 94

About the Author

JEFFREY M. TOGMAN is Assistant Professor of Political Science at Seton Hall University. Professor Togman's work has been published in such journals as *Oxford International Review, Conflict Management and Peace Science,* and *PS: Political Science and Politics.*